Penguin Books
Dear Doctor Hip Pocrates

Eugene Schoenfeld was born in 1935 in New York City.
He has worked at the Albert Schweitzer Hospital in
Lamberene, Gabon, both as an extern in 1959 and 1960,
and as a fully-qualified doctor in 1965–6. It was here
that a witch-doctor introduced him to a root called
iboga, used by the Gabonese to obtain hallucinogenic
experiences. From 1966–70 he was a Staff Physician on
the Student Health Service of the University of
California at Berkeley and has since 1967 been attached
to the Center for Special Problems in San Francisco, a
publicly operated psychiatric clinic with emphasis on
problems involving sex and drugs.

D1418737

Dr Eugene Schoenfeld

Dear Doctor Hip Pocrates

Advice Your Family Doctor
Never Gave You

Penguin Books

Penguin Books Ltd, Harmondsworth,
Middlesex, England
Penguin Books Australia Ltd, Ringwood,
Victoria, Australia

First published in the U.S.A. by Grove Press, Inc., 1968
Published in Penguin Books 1973
Reprinted 1973
Copyright © Eugene Schoenfeld, 1968

Made and printed in Great Britain by
C. Nicholls & Company Ltd
Set in Monotype Plantin

This book is dedicated to my family:
Mom, Dad, Barbara, Frank, friends

Dedication No. 2
To my readers and to the United States Post Office

Table of Contents

Note to the Penguin Edition

The manner in which Dr Schoenfeld advises his correspondents is so essentially his own that it would be impertinent to attempt to 'translate' it for the benefit of readers in this country. I have limited my direct interference to Anglicizing the spelling and to substituting English equivalents where possible for the brand names of drugs which do not seem to be available in this country. I have left unchanged the selection of questions and the answers given by Dr Schoenfeld but, where this has seemed necessary, I have added footnotes which provide information relevant to life this side of the Atlantic. On the latter pages, which deal almost exclusively with questions about drugs of addiction or dependence, I have commented very little. The drug scene in this country is still – quantitatively at least, and I think qualitatively also – very different from that in the United States, particularly in California. For my part I hope that this state of affairs will continue and that however amusing and instructive some of Dr Schoenfeld's remarks may be they will not prove to be an encouragement to readers of his entertaining book to do more than read!

Douglas Robb, M.R.C.S., L.R.C. P

Preface by Joel Fort, M.D.

Early in 1967, a serious 32-year-old staff physician sought my advice at San Francisco's Center for Special (sex, drug, etc.) Problems. I had founded the Center and was then directing it. The young doctor wanted my opinion about a column he was considering writing for the Berkeley *Barb*. His concerns at that time illustrate well the establishmentarian hypocrisy and irrationality forced upon all of us: 'respectable' people like physicians are not supposed to involve themselves in controversial subjects such as sex and drugs, or to 'advertise' themselves in print. What would this mean for his career? Could these complex subjects be properly and humorously communicated to his future readers? Having become aware from Dr Eugene Schoenfeld's ideas and dress that he possessed the dangerous and un-American qualities of independence and nonconformity which were likely to make the column successful, I encouraged him to do it and not to worry about the Establishment's reaction. Perhaps then, or during a subsequent conversation, we discussed questions about oral-genital contact for which I suggested my only specific line for the column: 'It's all a matter of taste.'

The readers of this book and of his column are well aware of Dr Schoenfeld's subsequent success, not only in conventional square (or hip) terms, but as a man and writer. Thirty to forty letters a week from readers (more than 2,000 altogether since the column began on 24 March 1967); publication in ten 'underground' newspapers; and this book, which will be read widely. More important, he has provided public health education on taboo subjects about which most doctors and all health departments are frightened, and he has done this with clear, terse, funny language that reaches and grabs young and old.

More people buy the *Barb* (and the other papers for which he writes) because of the HIP POCRATES column than for any other reason.

How did someone who grew up in Miami Beach and whose home influences as judged by a letter from his mother ('People who ask those questions must be nuts – it makes me sick') must have been conventional American melting pot – how did he 'make it' to work with Albert Schweitzer in Africa and to develop this column? For most Americans, making it means going along with the system, conforming, brown-nosing, and back-slapping. For doctors: upholding the American Medical Association view that medical care is a privilege rather than a right, and opposing all social change. For psychiatrists: taking three years of conventional training in Freudian theory, ivory-couch psychotherapy, and Board examinations to demonstrate that they have sufficiently memorized conventional techniques of providing limited services to affluent middle- and upper-class out-patients and hospitalized psychotics while rejecting drug abusers, the poor, etc.

Dr Schoenfeld represents a new breed of psychiatrically oriented physicians who might find psychiatry residency training, Boards, etc. to be irrelevant and unimportant. He left his residency after six months because his column and the problems of society were more interesting and meaningful to him.

His administrative superiors had found his competence and public recognition quite disturbing. Their (and the profession's) loss is his and the public's gain.

Thus, the ideas of the Greek Hippocrates (and of the real hippie) – trust, confidentiality, and concern for human welfare – are being brought to the public in hip language. The questions that people have always wanted to ask their doctors or ministers (which, when they did ask, were never answered) now have a responsible listener. Whether discussing diets or deodorants, farting or fucking, alcohol or LSD, caffeine or marijuana, MACE or hepatitis, or just plain social commentary,

Eugene Schoenfeld is irreverent, direct, instructive, tuned in, and 'where it's at'. The pompous bureaucrat, the hypocritical citizen, the hung-up Puritan, the drug police, and the sex police will express disapproval (after devouring every word), but the young hippie, the suburban housewife, and the just plain sex-and-drug-preoccupied American sleeps better because HIP POCRATES is there.

Some will call it 'obscene' (Jack and Jill went up the hill to —) but beyond the eye and ear of the beholder we live in an obscene world dominated by apathy, ignorance, hate, amorality, and mediocrity.

Some will call it evil, notably the neo-Puritans who, as Mencken said, have 'the haunting fear that someone, somewhere may be happy'.

I call it mytholytic (destroying numerous sex and drug myths), informative and entertaining. Buy it and read it. Think about the society that produces such ignorance and misery. Oppose these evils. Move beyond drugs to reforming our society. Remember Auden's 'Unknown Citizen' – 'Was he free? Was he happy? The question is absurd: Had anything been wrong we certainly should have heard.'

Introduction

Shortly after returning from Africa in 1966, I was walking down Berkeley's Telegraph Avenue when I happened to meet a friend near the Mediterraneum coffee house. Somewhat furtively, my friend, an attorney, asked me what effect marijuana would have on a diabetic. I didn't know (no one does), but advised him that marijuana might possibly affect his insulin requirements.

During the rest of that year I was asked many similar questions by friends or acquaintances newly interested in drugs who were reluctant to speak of these matters to their own physicians. In some instances their questions about drugs (or sex) had been met with moralistic diatribes or stern warnings without reasons.

Later, I was on the staff of the Center for Special Problems, a San Francisco health department psychiatric clinic dealing with problems related to sex and drugs. Many patients had begun using harmful drugs because they had reason to disbelieve the warnings issued by so-called authorities – the heroin addicts, for example, who had not believed drugs could be physically addictive. After all, they had been told the same about marijuana and knew from their own experience and that of others that the drug was relatively innocuous and certainly not addictive. Strange gaps in sexual information also existed, even among well-educated individuals. For instance, the 23-year-old social worker who thought the umbilical cord of her unborn baby was attached to her own umbilicus. It seemed clear to me that artificial standards of morality and censorship were causing information to be withheld from people to the detriment of their mental and physical health.

The underground press provided a means of answering

even the most intimate and forbidden questions without fear that irate advertisers or pressure groups might restrict the printed material.

The letters in this book were selected because they were interesting, informative, or amusing. A few are obvious put-ons (though usually I can't tell the difference). Most have previously appeared in my weekly medical column HIP POCRATES and were originally seen in the pages of the underground press.

My special thanks are due to Max Scherr, editor of the Berkeley *Barb* (where HIP POCRATES first appeared), who suggested the name for the column. Art Kunkin, editor of the Los Angeles *Free Press*, caused HIP POCRATES to be syndicated by being the second newspaper to feature the column.

Invaluable aid and advice was given by Jeanne Cluff, Linda Goorland, James M. Harris, D.V.M., Leonard Micon, M.D., Barbara Quinn, Jacki and Al Ruby, Frank Schoenfeld, M.D., and G. Z. Yaavor. Many helpful suggestions were offered by the shiftless lot of mathematicians, musicians, physicians, and physicists who while away their leisure hours by the Strawberry Canyon Pool of the University of California, Berkeley campus.

Eugene Schoenfeld, M.D.
Berkeley, California

Cold Facts

I am a 26-year-old woman with much experience. The only way I have ever reached a climax is to get in a swimming pool or the sea or a bathtub with the water under sixty degrees F. and kick fast.

Then I can reach a climax once, get out, wait five to ten minutes, reach it again better, and if the water is real cold reach it up to four times.

I first feel the cold in my ankles. There are no thoughts that go with it. What's this?

I thought those were water smudges on your letter but wasn't certain until after reading it. Many women experience sexual pleasure or can even reach a climax merely by rubbing the thighs together. All female orgasms are achieved by clitoral stimulation, directly or indirectly.

In *Human Sexual Response*, Masters and Johnson record the result of their pioneering research in the physiology of sex. Hundreds of individuals, prostitutes and university professors, their spouses and lovers, volunteered for the experiments. All varieties of sexual acts were carefully recorded on colour movie film and tape recorder. An ingenious transparent plastic penis was designed which contained a movie lens, thus allowing the researchers to record changes in the colour of the vagina during intercourse and orgasm.

The female subject could alter the speed, position, and depth of thrust of the penis-lens. Masters and Johnson proved that the difference between clitoral and vaginal orgasms is a myth.

This myth was popularized by Freud, who, after all, had failings like any other mortal. Unfortunately his followers, now become disciples, quote his words as if they were the pronouncements of an infallible almighty god. The Freudian temples are called Analytic Institutes.

Premature Ejaculation

I have great difficulty in prolonging my climax in intercourse long enough for my wife's satisfaction – or even my own, for that matter. Is there some method or medication I can use to delay orgasm?

'Premature' ejaculation is a common problem usually cured by time and experience with one's partner.

Since prehistoric man discovered alcohol, he has known that certain drugs may alter sexual performance.

Some drugs, prescribed for other purposes, may have as a side effect (usually undesirable) difficulty in achieving orgasm. One of the most commonly prescribed tranquillizers, Melleril, has this effect in some individuals.

Amphetamines commonly make sexual arousal and fulfilment more difficult to achieve.

To the best of my knowledge, these side effects have not been used to treat problems of premature ejaculation. The drawbacks of using a tranquillizer or amphetamine might outweigh any advantages.

Both categories of drugs are available by prescription only. A physician can best decide treatment in individual cases.

Some men find that the application of an anaesthetic ointment to the head and shaft of the penis half an hour or so prior to intercourse allows them to prolong their coital experience. Nupercainal is one such anaesthetic ointment available without a prescription.

Use of a condom ('prophylactic', 'rubber') will also decrease penile sensitivity. But many men and women find this barrier to ultimate togetherness objectionable.

Working Out

I am 45 years of age, unmarried, and in excellent physical condition, which I maintain by working out weekly at the YMCA. My problem is that every so often while doing chin-ups, I have an orgasm. This prevents me from finishing my workout, but after relaxing in the hot room I seem to feel better than ever.

Nevertheless, there are physical and moral implications which I would like to have cleared up, i.e.

1) Is this physically harmful?

2) Since I usually know it is going to happen and continue the chin-ups anyway, would the Catholic Church consider this masturbation and therefore a sin?

I suspect there is something about this situation which arouses you consciously or unconsciously. Aside from being unable to continue your workout, no physical harm seems possible. But you should consult your own physician who may wish to refer you for psychiatric consultation.

I am not widely renowned as a Catholic theologian, so suggest you consult a priest in order to find out whether the situation you mention is considered sinful in the eyes of the Church.

Smothered by Affection

Would you comment please on the following description of coital-mechanics:

During coitus, that moment just this side of orgasm (hers), the object is to somehow stop up all of her orifices. This, I am assured, will heighten the ecstasy of orgasm. Ecstasy aside, do you see possible harm in such 'stoppage' – fittingly called 'smother-fucking'?

Dear Smotherer:
Remember that it's a rare person who can hold his breath more than three or four minutes, so timing is important. Asphyxiation aside, one wonders about the means. In any case, many female readers will be left breathless by your letter.

Withdrawn

I do not appear to have a clitoris. Naturally, due to this fact, I do not have much of an orgasm, either.

What is a withdrawn clitoris? I have heard this term used and wonder if this is applicable in my case. Is there anything that can be done in such a case? Is this at all common?

I would appreciate any help or information you can give.

The clitoris is usually described as a miniature penis. (All genital organs, male and female, internal and external, have their counterparts in the opposite sex: nipples in the male, for example.) Like the penis, it has a glans, a shaft, and a foreskin. But the sole functions of the clitoris are sexual arousal and gratification.

Clitorises vary in size normally, and clinical research has shown that size does not determine sexuality or the capacity for sexual gratification. The same, of course, is true of penis size.

During periods of sexual excitement, the clitoris increases in size due to engorgement (with blood) of the glans. At the same time, the entire clitoris is retracted to a higher position on the symphysis pubis (the bone cushioned by the soft, fleshy mons pubis). Just before orgasm, there may be a fifty-per-cent reduction in the length of the clitoris due to retraction of the clitoral shaft.

This normal retraction of the clitoris away from the vaginal opening would be undesirable if direct stimulation by the penis were necessary for sexual gratification. But stimulation of the clitoris during intercourse is almost always indirect, the result of penile traction on the labia minora or inner lips of the vaginal orifice. This means of clitoral stimulation during intercourse is the same regardless of the coital position or minor variations in the location and size of the clitoris.

If the clitoris did not retract during intercourse, there would be many bitchy women because the line between stimulation and irritation is as thin as a methedrine head.

Clinical observations of women masturbating indicate that concentrating on the clitoris alone during sexual foreplay may be too much of a good thing. During automanipulation women stimulate the entire mons area, and if they stimulate the clitoris directly they give their favours to the shaft rather than the glans.

To be blunt, a thigh, knee, or heel of the hand may be better appreciated than a digit.

Beauty or Beastly?

Would you offer a medical or other comment on a woman who adamantly refuses to do sex as it's done in dogdom? Is man really the only animal who does 'it' face to face?

A prominent red-bearded veterinarian has doggedly come to our aid. His first reaction was to thank you on behalf of his wife and himself for bringing to their attention this exotic new 'face-to-face' position used by some humans. He also offers the information that chimpanzees, gorillas, and monkeys sometimes copulate face to face but they usually perform that act 'doggy' style.

Perhaps your lady friend is so enamoured of you she can't bear not looking at your face. Some people don't like things done behind their backs so you might consider using a mirror, which would also give her a new perspective on love. Besides, mirrors can be a great turn-on.

Above all, your friend should be assured that you will not force her to fornicate on crowded street corners. Nor will cold water be splashed over the two of you.

There is no 'right' or 'proper' way to make love. Consenting, mature individuals ought to be able to make love however and whenever they like so long as they do not intrude upon the rights and privacy of others. An aversion to one of the many ways of making love ought to be treated with compassion, understanding, and above all, patience, since changes in sexual patterns may occur even at a relatively advanced sexual age. People who feel secure with each other, who are certain they won't be put down in any way by their partner(s) are the most free and relaxed in love.

Victorian women were supposed to lie placidly thinking about housework or hats until the dreadful deed was done. Two views prevail today. One is to concentrate on loving the person. The other holds that the act itself should be paramount. The most fulfilling and difficult way is to do both.

Multiple Orgasms

I've heard of women who can climax two or three times in the course of one extended act of love. Is there anything I can do to acquire this ability? I anticipate that you might advise me to reach my first orgasm quickly in order not to use up too much energy. I've tried this and I'm usually turned off.

There are women who can have four or five orgasms or more during one extended act of love. But who can say if they are more satisfied than a woman who has one which is totally fulfilling? We're back to the quantity vs quality question again.

Many women reach orgasm only through automanipulation and some not at all.

A lengthy coital episode is helpful in some cases. Perhaps there are readers with suggestions presently unknown to medical science.

Here's a comment to your question by a University of Miami medical student:

'Have you had a blood test recently? Perhaps you have a rare condition causing your blood cells to be oval rather than round. Camels are the only mammals normally having oval red blood cells so you may be descended from a dromedary. If so, you are destined to be at most a two-humped girl.'

Anal Intercourse

Dear Dr Schoenfeld:
Anal intercourse is, for me, a far more satisfactory means of obtaining multiple orgasms than vaginal intercourse and I have been enjoying the former act for nearly fifteen years, averaging no less than three times weekly. There have been no signs of haemorrhoids, no irregularity, and since the first few times I experimented, no pain. There is considerable pleasure for me during the act, and after the emission of semen I enjoy a five or ten minute period of utter serenity.

Sincerely,
Linda G—

Here's a shitty question for you: Can haemorrhoids be caused by anal intercourse, and if so, can you say what the frequency and force would be to cause them?

Thank You

What are the dangers involved in anal intercourse and how may they be overcome? I am not a homosexual, but I do enjoy an occasional piece of asshole.

23

Because of the many letters I receive from males and females concerning anal intercourse, I recently consulted a noted proctologist. His opinion is that anal intercourse is not physically harmful when done in moderation. When performed frequently (and don't ask me to define frequent) there may be a tendency for the passive partner to develop earlier in life conditions usually found a decade or two later – such as haemorrhoids and a loosening of the anal sphincter or muscles controlling the anus.

Theoretically, one would expect a high incidence of urinary tract infections in the active partner because E. coli bacteria, which most commonly cause urinary tract infections, are normally found in the rectum. But clinically, no increase in urinary tract infections in active partners has been observed. Soap and water cleansing of the penis and hands will help prevent bladder infections in the female if vaginal intercourse follows anal intercourse.

Rectal VD is a real danger of anal intercourse because the carrier usually has no symptoms. Both gonorrhoea and syphilis may be found.

Sodomy (a legal term for anal intercourse) is a felony crime in most states, punishable by long prison terms. The name is derived from the Biblical city destroyed because of its 'wickedness'. But what were they doing in Gomorrah?*

Double the Pleasure

Dear Dr Schoenfeld:
Recently my husband and I have been attending group sexual parties and I have submitted to 'double-screwing', i.e., one penis in my vagina and a second in my rectum simultaneously. It isn't easy to accomplish but when it is I am transported into another world!

*Sodomy is an arrestable offence in the UK, and here too is punishable by long prison terms.

For me to reach climax a half dozen times is not unusual and each orgasm is more gratifying than the one preceding it.

Question: Is there any possibility of injury to the wall separating the two cavities? The only discomfort I feel is at the first penetration of my anus after the penis is already inserted in my vagina, and this pain is quite brief and not at all agonizing. A subquestion: Is the use of Nupercainal as a lubricant for anal intercourse harmful in any way?

Sincerely yours,
Claudia—

The wall between the rectum and the vagina, the recto-vaginal septum, is sometimes torn during an unexpectedly rapid childbirth. But this injury is rare. The means of injury you suggest do not seem likely to cause such a tear. Stretching of the anal sphincter, or muscles controlling the anus, is possible with 'excessive' anal intercourse.

Nupercainal and other anaesthetic ointments are used for the relief of pain due to haemorrhoids. They also may be used to desensitize the penis, thus enabling some men to prolong coitus before ejaculation. Your use of a topical anaesthetic may have an unexpected (and undesired) effect on your male friends.

Sneezes and Orgasms

I've heard that the intensity of a woman's sneeze is somehow comparable to the intensity of her orgasm – a very convulsive sneeze, a very convulsive orgasm. A sexologist has said this observation is not to be sneezed at. Would you please comment?

Seems to me I've heard the same. I'm certain there are many who would be willing to join in a research project to settle this question.

God Bless You for your letter.

Regarding orgasms and sneezes.

What can be said of beings who frequently attempt to abort their sneezes by blocking the nostrils? I know of several such 'abortionists' who also have weak orgasms – weak as defined by either themselves or their partners.

Blocking the nostrils while sneezing may cause a ruptured eardrum because of greatly increased air pressure. The Eustachian tubes are the connecting airways between the nasal passages and ears. Before aeroplane cabins were pressurized, it was necessary to yawn or swallow when ascending or descending in order to equalize pressure of the air in the ears and the outside air.

Research on the relationship between sneezes and orgasms continues and is soon expected to reach a climax.

More on sneezes. A medical student from the University of Cincinnati has apparently been nosing about for information on this vital question. He sent me a photocopy of page 748 from Ham's *Histology*, fifth edition, a textbook widely used in medical schools. The author states that the nasal passages are lined with erectile tissue very similar to that found in the penis and notes the case of a sixteenth-century youth who sneezed each time he saw a pretty girl.

To those who may still raise their noses to the possibility of a relationship between the genital and nasal systems, he points out that in much of the animal kingdom sexual stimulation is dependent upon smell. This applies also to man.

Several patients have reported relief from nasal congestion following sexual intercourse. No prescription is required.

Seminal Fluid

What is the composition of human semen? Is it particularly rich in hormones? What would be the effect of swallowing a small amount nearly daily? (I like the taste.) Would there be a significantly different effect on male and female systems?

Human semen is largely composed of sperm and secretions from the prostate gland. The Cowper and Littré glands of the penis also secrete a small amount of fluid, probably to lubricate the urethra of the penis.

The usual volume of ejaculated semen is from 3–5 ml. (millilitre) or about the contents of a teaspoon. Each millilitre of semen contains 60 to 120 million spermatozoa. Testosterone, the male hormone produced by the testes, is released directly into the bloodstream and is not a constituent of semen. The effect of your swallowing semen nearly daily would be more easily detected in your friend than in you. But no large-scale scientific investigation into this matter has been carried out.

It is my obligation to remind you of the stiff penalties provided by law for the 'crime' of fellatio.*

Detective Work

In a question about swallowing semen you said that this practice 'would be more easily detected in your friend (the source) than in you (the swallower).' How can you tell?

By the twinkle in his eye.

A Fluid Household

(The following letter, like the preceding letter about semen, is from Orinda, California. Orinda!)

I am currently trying to get pregnant after taking birth-control pills for three years. The problem is thusly:

*This is not a crime in the UK.

I live in a rather fluid household. Besides my lawful, legal-type husband, there is almost always one additional man around and frequently there are several. I would like my first child to be my husband's but monogamy at our house is difficult and not particularly desirable to any of us. What is the best method of temporary contraception that won't interfere with my husband's sperm but will reduce the chances of anybody else's?

We'll use condoms if necessary but that's a big drag generally. I have been using foam but there seem to be drawbacks to the two brands available: 1) I seem to develop some outlandish internal temperature, at least it feels that way. Several people say that their penises (peni?) seem to heat up to about 240 degrees F. when the foam is properly injected. 2) I've noticed that after using the foam, I get very sore. Like I can't sit down comfortably even. 3) While none of my not-husbands have gotten me pregnant, neither has my husband. How long does it take foam to disperse?

Your plight is a difficult one but I will try to answer your questions. Some women do have discomfort after using vaginal foams; this seems to be a local reaction similar to a cosmetic rash. The great heat noted by you and your friends might be generated by friction, but I suspect that their discomfort and yours is caused by a local allergy to the foam you are using.

Sperm may be alive and groping about one or two days after intercourse. Vaginal foams are usually effective in killing the sperm on contact but do not always work. A fresh application of foam is required each time intercourse occurs. The dispersal time is inconstant, depending on the individual.

In your circumstances the best way to conceive your husband's child would be the use of a diaphragm. The diaphragm could then be used at all times except between the tenth and eighteenth days of your menstrual cycle. These days should be reserved for your ever-loving lawful husband. Don't borrow a girlfriend's diaphragm. Have it fitted by a gynaecologist.

Orinda and Oneida

I am inquiring as to whether the community of Orinda is in any way related to the Oneida community established by John Noyes. Are the Orinda's principles similar to the Oneida's abolition of monogamy?

If so, I would like to hear more about this in future articles. If not, what are the principles of these people and where may I find more information about them?

Orinda is a San Francisco Bay Area suburb nestled back of the Berkeley hills. The principles of some of its inhabitants may resemble those of the Oneida community (the people of the Oneida community not only abolished monogamy but practised a kind of birth control, coitus interruptus), but so far they are not yet incorporated into the town charter. In fact, there is no town charter. For further information about the characteristics of Orindians, write to the Contra Costa County Chamber of Commerce.

Virgin Births

(Here's another letter from the endlessly fascinating community of Orinda.)
Could you please tell me if it is possible to become pregnant without coitus if ejaculation occurred outside the vagina?

Pregnancy without coitus is possible if semen is at or near the entrance to the vagina. This may occur even if a girl is wearing underpants, according to some now well-informed female sources.

Perhaps this helps to explain the phenomenon of virgin births. But it still seems a poor way to become pregnant.

Ready

(The following letter is from Los Angeles.)

I am 30, single, and after years of having puritanical ideas of pre-marital sex, am now prepared for sex with a woman for whom I have affection. However, I am hesitant to 'go all the way' because: 1) of past puritanical conditioning; 2) of my inexperience, the awkwardness of my physical contribution in the initial sex experience; 3) of fear of being verbally rejected by a woman to whom I've explained my celibacy.

How can I overcome these fears and experience the sex act that I need and want so dearly?

You might consider moving to Orinda. And if I didn't think you were really concerned that is all I would have to say. I am not certain from your letter whether you have a particular woman in mind; if so, she is ready also by this time. You would probably be more comfortable in your initial experience with a mature woman who, rather than putting you down for inexperience, would be delighted to instruct you. Don't worry about the mechanics of your first sexual experience. It's all programmed.

Humbug

Have you ever heard of something called a 'hum' job? During fellatio or cunnilingus one vigorously hums a tune such as 'Jingle Bells'. What do you think of this?

Hmmm. Merry Christmas.

Razzing

The reader who wrote you about the 'hum-job' divulged a rare and beautiful secret indeed; but have you heard of a 'razzberry job'? It is similar to the 'hum-job' (humming during fellatio and/or cunnilingus), but instead of humming one executes a loud and vibratory 'razzberry' at the appropriate moment – which is determined by individual experimentation.

It is important to maintain good contact while 'razzing' so that the vibrations are not all lost to the air.

I think a 'razzberry' is the same as a 'Bronx cheer'. But are you giving us a snow job?

Incest

I need some fast advice from you. For the past three and a half years I have had regular sexual intercourse with my father and my younger brother – while on the pill, of course. Something was wrong with one month's supply and I cannot tell which is the father.

Will I have a defective child? Should I go for an abortion? Both prospective fathers want me to have the baby. We have no mother or younger children to worry about.

Children of closely related parents are more likely to have inherited birth defects than when the parents are not related. But if no hereditary diseases are present, the child should be normal. The most likely cause for this pregnancy is not something wrong with the birth-control pills, but failure to take them as directed. California and other states permit a legal abortion in cases of incest.*

Does your family pray together too?

*Incest is a criminal offence in the UK, punishable by imprisonment.

(The following letter was received from the Los Angeles area.)

I have just read the question of the girl who seemed concerned over having her father's baby. Allow me to say that I have gone through the experience and that Linda is a wonderful healthy little girl whom Daddy and I both adore. We have lived together since my mother's death three years ago and Linda is now fourteen months old. I think I could never really love another man except my father.

Masturbation

Dear Dr Schoenfeld:
When giving a physical exam, can a doctor tell if a female patient masturbates?
If it is not possible to be sure in the case of a teenager, is it possible to tell if it is a habit of long standing in a 20- or 30-year-old unmarried woman?
Thank you for your serious consideration of this question so difficult to ask.

Scared, Ignorant, Alone

There is a story about a little boy who was found masturbating and was told he would go blind unless he stopped. 'Well,' he pleaded, 'can I do it until I need eyeglasses?'

Doctors cannot tell from physical examination whether or not their patients masturbate. This is true regardless of the age of the patient or the length of time he or she has been masturbating.

There is no evidence that masturbation is physically or mentally harmful, whatever its frequency.

Menstrual Cramp Treatment

A girl I know tells me she finds masturbation relieves her menstrual cramps. Is she putting me and herself on?

There is valid scientific evidence that sexual activity during menstruation relieves menstrual discomfort for many women. Some use automanipulation specifically for this purpose.

Backaches and cramping associated with menstruation are often relieved by sexual activity. Masters and Johnson (whose pioneering research was published in *Human Sexual Response*) filmed the cervix during orgasm and found an increased rate of menstrual flow, probably due to contractions of the uterus.

Lopsided?

Is there anything specially abnormal with having one breast slightly larger than the other? I find it inhibiting at times, though my lover says he doesn't even notice it. Is there any way to balance the situation?

Differences in the two halves of the body are found in everyone. Few people have shoe sizes exactly alike for both feet.

Even the two sides of a face are different. Movie stars, for example, often prefer one profile shot over another.

Breasts are rarely exactly alike in size and shape. Your lover probably enjoys the variation; perhaps he even has a favourite.

My secretary, almost never at a loss for an answer to a question, said in all sincerity, 'I thought it was because guys liked one more than the other.' I told her one must learn not to rely solely on subjective experiences.

Her solution to breasts of disproportionate sizes was to wait until a baby is born, then nurse more from the smaller breast.

This theory was supported by the following letter received from a member of the La Leche League, an organization which provides information about breast feeding:

If you nurse your baby from the larger breast, it will remain larger and even increase its seniority. The thing to do is to nurse more on the smaller side. That will tend to even things up during lactation.

The more milk the baby takes from the breast, the more it will produce. The trouble with being very lopsided is that the bra will be tight on the larger side and tight bras cause plugged milk ducts.

Occasionally there is a truly noticeable and perhaps embarrassing difference between the two breasts. If so, the situation may be handled by a plastic surgeon.

Abundance

I am a girl (23) who has an unusual bustline problem – too much! I'm 5' 5", 120 lbs., wear a size 10 dress and have a 36D bustline.

I wouldn't mind it so much if it weren't quite so droopy – without a bra I closely resemble those Neolithic Venuses on the cover of the latest Scientific American.

I didn't start wearing a bra until a year after I should have and didn't wear one at night until I was about 20. Weight loss only makes things worse. Consequently, I'm quite unattractive in the nude.

I've been trying exercises for the past couple of months but it hasn't helped a bit as the problem isn't the muscles but the skin. What I'd like to know is: 1) Would plastic surgery help? 2) How much would it cost? 3) If I did have surgery, would it permit me to go bra-less occasionally – if not I might as well forget the whole thing right now.

> Yours truly,
> The Neolithic Fertility Goddess

P.S. *While we're on the subject of breasts – one of my nipples is constantly hard, the other is always soft, even when I'm turned on – is this abnormal?*

Those Neolithic Venuses looked pretty good to me. Who told you you're unattractive in the nude?

Surgery is sometimes performed to reduce the size of very large sagging breasts. The cosmetic results vary depending upon the breasts, the skill of the surgeon, and fate. A certain amount of scarring is inevitable. Your county medical society or nearest medical school can recommend a plastic surgeon to you.

Fees vary considerably but you can count on spending about $1,000 for the procedure. Afterwards, you could go bra-less but changes in the body, including breast tissue, are an inevitable part of the life process.*

Having one nipple erect and the other soft when aroused is perfectly normal. But wearing a bra to bed won't be of benefit to your breasts and may turn off potential arousers.

Keeping in Shape

My wife is concerned about her breasts drooping after our baby is born and wants to know if they can be brought back into shape; she plans to breast-feed the baby. This concerns me too, since I am as breast-brainwashed as the next American male.

After the birth of your baby, your wife should exercise daily to maintain and improve the muscle tone of all her body. These

* Her general practitioner would be able to advise this reader and, if it seemed desirable, refer her to a plastic surgeon. Unless it can be regarded as medically necessary, not all plastic surgeons are prepared to undertake this sort of surgery under the N H S, and she might have to be prepared to pay for it herself.

exercises should include the pectoral muscles, which help give support to the breasts. Breast-fed is best fed. Groove with your wife and baby doing their beautiful thing.

Your nearest YWCA or Red Cross chapter should have classes and/or booklets providing information about the proper exercises for your wife.*

Predicting the Future

My girlfriend, who has fine, shapely breasts, doesn't wear a bra any more and I love it and so does she. We were wondering, however, what effect this will have on her breasts, e.g., in ten or twenty years.

If your girlfriend's fine, shapely breasts are of 'normal' size, regular exercise to strengthen her pectoral muscles would be of more benefit to her than a bra. The shape of a woman's breasts will change as she matures. Besides, in ten or twenty years she may have ten or twenty children.

Quantity and Quality

Can anything be done to increase penis size at the age of about 20? I feel I am underdeveloped and have always felt a little inadequate because of it.

When I was a high-school student, a friend felt he had the same problem. Each day he would tie a weight to his penis, swinging it like a pendulum and gradually increasing the weight. He worked his way up to ten or fifteen pounds, setting some sort of record in masochism, but his member remained unchanged except for some rope burns.

* In the UK, the ante-natal or post-natal clinic will be able to advise a woman on suitable exercises.

Only in rare instances is there a real problem of physical incompatibility between male and female. When this does occur, the problem is likely to be as illustrated by the remark of a local topless dancer, 'I'd rather be tickled than choked.'

Sexually experienced and mature women will tell you that quality, not quantity, is where it's at when making love. If a woman feels she is truly wanted and loved as demonstrated by your words and sexual foreplay, she is not going to measure your penis.

The thrust of my answer, and this is not a tongue-in-cheek reply, is that the measure of a person and his sexuality is not the size of his genitals.

Unsatisfied

Your comments in the column regarding penis size were interesting and perhaps (but I doubt it) reassuring to the questioner; however, they failed to answer the question. Please indicate what, if anything, could be done to increase penis size at the age of 20, or younger or older.

If gonadotropic (gonad stimulating) hormones are given before or during puberty there will be an increase in the size of the penis as well as an intensification of the secondary sexual characteristics such as facial and body hair. But these hormones will also cause closing of the epiphyses or growth centres of the long bones, thus stopping vertical growth of the individual.

Urologists say nothing can be done to increase penis size after maturation. Something can be done to end the phallacy (pardon pun) that penis or breast size is somehow related to sexual prowess. Some of the most sexually hung-up men and women are very well hung.

Satisfied

Dear Dr Schoenfeld:

I doubt that penis enlargement is part of any curriculum, therefore your lack of information is understandable and unfortunate. This information has been available to mankind for at least a few thousand years.

I know whereof I speak because I accomplished this and am, at this writing, 60 years old. The method requires no drugs or instruments or surgery.

You are a doctor and can evaluate this. I would not recommend this process to anyone because there is danger of bruising unless done under supervision. If you require further information, print your question in your column.

Sincerely,
Gilbert —

I agree that medical knowledge exists outside of 'accepted' medical channels. But physicians are rightly cautious about new and unknown modes of treatment, especially when harm may be done to people. We also are wary of quackery which feeds upon the disparity between present knowledge and the needs or wishes of humans. However, my curiosity is piqued. What is your method and how did you discover it?

(Note: The 60-year-old gentleman replied that five years previously, he had over a nine-month period added two inches to the length and nearly doubled the circumference of his penis. He described the method but did not give additional information.)

Bouncing Baby

I would like some advice on fucking during pregnancy. Is there any position that will not hurt a pregnant woman during the later months? Please answer soon.

Most gynaecologists advise against intercourse in the last month of pregnancy. But your own doctor undoubtedly has his own theory. By that time the only feasible position for many couples is face to back.

In the 1940s some scientists of the Dianetics school wondered what effect intercourse had on the psyche of the unborn child. Imagine the foetus floating in warmth and darkness. Suddenly he is subjected to thumping, buffeting, and other phenomena. Are there any readers who remember?

(Note: Physicians differ in their opinion of sexual intercourse during the latter stages of pregnancy. But there's no doubt in the mind of the woman who wrote the following delightful letter.)

Hip:
Isn't intercourse position during pregnancy a matter of individual anatomy? We never had to switch to the Dog Position, even in the final month. The face-to-face positions were perfectly comfortable.

Our doctor believes in full sex relations until labour begins. What a boon to pregnant womanhood! No more must we complain 'the ninth month is longer than the other eight'.

Labour was good and the baby does not have a flat head. He loves bumpy stroller rides and judging by his banging on the highchair today, he has a fine sense of rhythm.

Boost for Yoga

To attempt to become an autofellatioist – would this be stretching things too far?

I think it may be stretching narcissism too far.

(Note: The following unedited letter was received from a Los Angeles man in response to the preceding question and answer.)

Dear Doctor:
The letter regarding 'autofellatio' intregs me. I never heard the word before altho I was a devoted practioner of that glorious pastime for years & years.

Let's start at the beginning. When I was not more than five years old I had a favourite place in our woodshed where I could sit & try to satisfy a strong desire to kiss the head of my penis (erected). I tried quite often for years and when I was twelve made it just on the tip. As time went on I got better until at about fourteen I could take the whole head in my mouth & roll my tongue around it. I can't remember the first time I got it off but not long thereafter.

From then on it was an almost daily ritual – loving, kissing, biting, & teasing. If I did not have at least a half hour of privacy I would not bother. Some days twice and on occasion three times. My, my my! in all of Heaven's creation there is no pleasure like this.

I married when I was forty-eight (dam fool) & never had enough privacy very often so gradually got out of practice (stiff back). Got my last one at fifty-eight – if I die this evening I go willingly. I've sur had more than my share – thousands & thousands.

Every word of this is true So help me God.
As for narcissism – I wonder if there is a healthy male in this

world who has not wished he could lean over & kiss his erection smack on the head as I have done?

I have met two men in my time who said they could.

Surprise!

Doctor:
Right after our climax was reached, I touched my lover's testicles. He reacted in what I then thought was just further ecstasy, but later he said that it was very painful. But just at that moment he said that if I had done it earlier, it wouldn't have hurt at all.

Why does that happen? I am not overly experienced yet, so I would like to know. Could you send me a reply instead of printing one? He reads your column every week and I want him to be surprised.

> *Thank you,*
> *Susan —*

Dear Susan:
There are many things in love as well as in medicine which may be learned only by experience. You have mentioned one of them.

Touching the testicles before orgasm is one of the ways a woman may greatly excite her lover: in fact, it is a way of hastening the orgasm of the male. Many women never learn this so your lover is fortunate that you have.

But for some reason, touching the testicles just after orgasm often gives an unpleasant sensation. This is sometimes true also of intercourse immediately after a climax has been reached.

As you spend more time with your lover you will discover the things which please both of you. And so long as both of you agree, there is nothing you can do that is wrong or shameful.

> Sincerely,
> Eugene Schoenfeld, M.D.

Habit or Hang-up?

As I understand it, most women pad themselves with tissues or towels after intercourse, and postpone washing up till morning. This practice has always been repugnant to me, so I developed the habit of washing up immediately after every intercourse. My husband claims that this is just another one of my hang-ups. What do you have to say on that?

A non-random sample has revealed that most women do not pad themselves with tissues or towels after intercourse – if they do it's only to avoid staining the sheets. Nor is it necessary to wash immediately after intercourse. Perhaps your husband wishes you to stay with him awhile after making love. That's a very important time, you know.

(Note: The following is a letter from what I believe to be another 'non-random sample'.)

Dear Hip Pocrates:
I not only pad myself with Kleenex, but also usually insert a tampon in my vagina as soon as I can before going to sleep. The first is indeed to keep the sheets clean; the second lets me get a good night's sleep. Before I thought of this, I used to wake up two or three times during the night as I 'leaked'; now the tampon takes care of everything. Granted, it's an expensive habit – but it's worth it.

Sincerely,
J.C.

P.S. *My boyfriend doesn't seem to mind.*

Flying High

A surgeon has recently informed me that he has been able to cure his sexual impotency through kite-flying. This idea came

to him after reading a brief article by Sandor Ferenczi entitled
'The Kite As Symbol of Erection' (found in the Selected Papers
of S. Ferenczi, Vol. 2).

What comment have you to make about this?

I recently gave a talk to a discussion group of the East Bay
Sexual Freedom League. When I read this letter to illustrate a
common problem of males, S F L Director Tom Palmer asked
where the kite-string had been attached. Strangely enough
there was a Sandor Ferenczi who did write such a paper.

Impotency is the inability to have an erection or the inability to have an orgasm. Though impotency tends to increase
after the age of 40 it is not necessarily a normal part of the
ageing process. As a medical student I treated an 83-year-old
man who had suffered a heart attack shortly after masturbating. He had recently been discharged from another hospital
after prostate surgery and was just making sure all was intact.

Usually no physical cause can be found for impotency
though occasionally a surgically correctable circulatory defect
may be found. Males of any age concerned with an impotency
problem should consult their physicians. Often a course of
psychiatric treatment is beneficial.

Painful Decision

*Do you think excessive sexual activity leads to high blood-
pressure? Will a diminution of sexual activity lessen high blood-
pressure? And do you think men can really fuck themselves to
death?*
P.S. *Delaying a lot of decisions until I hear from you.*

First of all, I don't know what is meant by 'excessive' sexual
activity. What seems normal to one person may seem like
satyrism to another.

During intercourse and automanipulation, blood-pressure is definitely raised, but this normal physiologic change is temporary. Restriction of sexual activity in the case of abnormally high blood-pressure or following a heart attack is a decision to be made in consultation with one's physician. An important consideration is that such restrictions might add to emotional tensions, thus further complicating the problem.

Several well-known public figures have died in bed following sexual activities, peacefully, one assumes, but not in their sleep. The cause of death is usually due to a heart attack or rupturing of an aneurism (an outpouching of a blood vessel). But sex is not as dangerous as we've been led to believe. Any strenuous activity or even nervous tension might be the immediate cause of such deaths.

Dangerous

I am an inexperienced and shy teen-age girl, aged 16. I know the facts of life but not how to put them to use. Please give me some advice on how to have intercourse. I've never had any sexual experience but my friends tell me it's groovy.

'*Missing Out*'

My favourite occupational therapist thinks your friends are right. But in most states your age makes you a hazardous commodity because of statutory rape provisions in the law. To help pass the time until your eighteenth birthday, when you will automatically and magically become mature enough to have sexual relations, I suggest you read *Love and Sex in Plain Language* by E. W. Johnston, Lippincott Co., $2.95.*

*In this country 16 is the age of sexual consent. A very helpful paperback which is available in this country is *The A.B.Z. of Love* by Sten and Inge Hegeler, published by Four Square Books.

Growth and Development

Does sexual intercourse limit in any way the physical growth of a maturing child, i.e., sexual intercourse experienced regularly by an adolescent who has not finished growing?

I have noticed no decrease in average stature among Berkeley youths.

Welcome Home

This is (for me) an embarrassing question to ask, but you seem to be my only source of information at the moment. What does 'blow' mean in sexual contact and can you describe the process? I have an idea but it's the method I don't know. Please . . . I'm serious about this.

P.S. *Please* hurry. *My boyfriend will be home in three weeks.*

The term you use is slang for fellatio or cunnilingus; it most usually refers to fellatio. Fellatio is the application of the mouth and tongue to the penis. Cunnilingus is the application of the tongue to the clitoris and vulvae. Both are by law felony crimes punishable by long prison terms. In Florida, these and other such crimes are covered by the general phrase 'the abominable crime against nature'.*

The perpetrators of these 'crimes', i.e., nearly everyone past puberty, are not prosecuted with much vigour by the authorities. One might even surmise that law-enforcement officials and their wives regularly commit these felonies.

P.S. I trust your boyfriend's homecoming will be a pleasant one.

*Neither of these are crimes in this country.

Flexible

During sexual intercourse, a few of my lovers have enjoyed raising both of my legs to my shoulders. I don't mind if the man is gentle. However, I have been told by a pimp-friend of mine that this can do harm to the uterus. Is this true?

I think your friend is excessively concerned about irritation of the cervix resulting from closer contact to the penis in this position. Yearly or twice yearly gynaecological examinations, including Pap or cancer smears, should be given to every woman. Don't worry about that particular position. It's recommended by skiers.

A Matter of Taste

Is anal-lingus (oh not to the exclusion of other 'linguistic doings') not to be enjoyed under any conditions?

There are more bacteria present in the mouth than in any other body orifice. Assuming there are no diseases present such as gonorrhoea, syphilis, typhoid, or infectious hepatitis, it just comes down to a matter of taste.

Geriatric Sex

Why is it there is so little sex interest on the part of older women past child-bearing age? They all seem fearful and become quite prudish.

One of the final passages in Huxley's *After Many a Summer* describes a couple well over 100 years old fornicating on the floor of a barred room. They are wrinkled, animal-like creatures who snarl and growl in a grotesque manner.

I mention this scene because it seems to sum up the commonly held attitude that sex in older individuals is somehow dirty. The expression 'dirty old man' is not quite funny (remember the 'clean' grandfather in *Hard Day's Night*).

About four years ago, *The Realist* had a cartoon showing an aged woman standing outside a home for the aged in a blinding blizzard. She clutched a newborn baby to her bosom and pleaded with the manager who blocked the doorway, his index finger righteously pointing to the snow and darkness. Beneath the cartoon was a news item reporting that the use of birth-control pills might postpone menopause to the sixties or seventies. Fortunately, obstetrical costs are covered by Medicare.

Sexuality at all ages is normal, common, and was so even before the introduction of hormones. Its expression in many older people seems to be modified or suppressed not so much by physiological factors as by the attitudes of our society.

Preventive Medicine

Could you list in order of effectiveness the various contraceptive methods?

The two most certain ways to prevent pregnancy are abstinence and the conscientious use of birth-control pills. Diaphragms combined with spermicidal jellies are *almost* always effective. Those able to use intrauterine devices (I U Ds) are most carefree but I U Ds have been expelled from the uterus unbeknownst to the user and can irritate the male member. Moreover, babies have been born gleefully grasping I U Ds. Condoms are a drag and may break. Companies producing vaginal foams and jellies claim them to be as effective as diaphragms but I know several children nicknamed Emko,

Preceptin, or Ortho. Rhythm is somewhat more effective than luck.*

News from Her Mother

My mom in New York keeps informing me of the latest anti-birth-control news. What have you heard about any ill effects from long-term use? Is it true that their use can bring on diabetes if there is a history of it in the family?

My mother hates sex so I don't know when to believe her.

A study recently conducted in England has indicated that women who use birth-control pills have, statistically, a slightly greater chance of getting blood clots in the arms, legs, and lungs than those who do not use the pills.

The new lower dose birth-control pills may reduce the possibility of blood-clot formation; they have only been recently introduced and results will not be known for several years.

In any case, the normal hazards of pregnancy are more common and more serious than those associated with the use of birth-control pills. There is no evidence that the 'pill' brings on diabetes mellitus, with or without a family history of the disease.

No ill effects from long-term use of contraceptive pills have been reported during the ten years they have been used.

Avoid Menstruation?

I would like to use birth-control pills to cut down the frequency of menstrual periods or to avoid them altogether. Do you have any advice on how long it is safe to postpone periods?

*I don't know about nicknames, but the English have coined a word for those who use the rhythm method: parents.

Some state mental hospitals use birth-control pills to stop or decrease the frequency of menstrual periods in mentally retarded or severely disturbed female patients who are unable to attend to their own needs. But relatively large doses of birth-control pills must be given to prevent 'break-through bleeding', a procedure certainly not recommended for normal females. It is only done because of the hygienic problem presented to the hospital nursing staff and is potentially dangerous.

My question is why this normal physiologic function of your body should be the cause of such distress to you. Menstruation has been described as but the uterus weeping for the loss of its child.

Getting the Pill

Are there any ways to get birth-control pills besides having to go to a doctor to get the prescription?

No and for good reason. The doctor will take a medical history and do a gynaecologic examination, including a Pap or cancer smear, to determine that there are no conditions which would be caused or made worse by taking birth-control pills. You should see your own physician or you may be eligible for care at your local health department or Planned Parenthood office. Doctors aren't so bad. Some of my best friends . . .*

*Most general practitioners in England are today prepared to prescribe contraceptive pills where they are called for; alternatively Family Planning Clinics are now in existence in almost every town. They are prepared to give advice and to prescribe for unmarried as well as married women. There are a few general practitioners who are unwilling for various reasons to assist their patients and who refuse either to provide or to agree to their obtaining contraceptive advice. It must not be forgotten that if anyone is not satisfied with his general practitioner's services, he has a perfect right to transfer to another

A Pill for Males?

Will there soon be birth-control pills for men?

Alas, I'm sorry to report that progress in this field appears to be flaccid. Recently, a drug was developed which did stop spermatogenesis. It also caused nausea and vomiting when alcohol was ingested, obviously a threat to the alcohol industry as well as an impediment to those who depend on alcohol for seduction.

Noting that heat seemed to retard spermatogenesis, some researchers directed volunteers to lower their testicles into 120 degree F. water baths, a method which had some success, though it is unlikely to be met with enthusiasm by the masses.

Undoubtedly, a pill or injection causing temporary sterility in males will eventually be developed. Meanwhile, make certain your girlfriend(s) can count.

Vasectomies

I was reading the unclassified ads in the L.A. Free Press today and kept coming across all those ads where some guy is looking for some chick to sleep with and he mentions that he has a vasectomy. Now I know what a vasectomy is but I'm curious to know the results, aside from sterility. Does it interfere with ejaculation? What are the pros and cons of the whole thing?

Vasectomies are simple surgical operations (often done in the doctor's office)* which cause sterility in males. The procedure

---

whose views may prove to be more sympathetic, or at least possible to live with.

*Vasectomy is becoming increasingly popular in this country, but it can at present only be done without charge in an NHS hospital if consists of anaesthetizing two small areas of the scrotum, making small incisions and severing both vas deferens, two spaghetti-like structures which transport sperm from the testicles.

Ejaculation and orgasm normally continue as before (sperm constitute only a part of the total seminal fluid volume).

The chief objection raised against vasectomies is that the resulting sterility is usually permanent. Too many cases arise in which a man later changes his mind and wishes to have children. Attempts to reunite the severed ends of the vas deferens are most often unsuccessful.

The Loop

What is the story on intrauterine devices? A doctor in Berkeley installed one for me but my doctor wants to take it out. The device has been in for two years now and during that time I have had two Pap smears, the results of which were negative for cancer. I did have two unusual spells of severe uterine cramps but nobody could attribute them to anything in particular.

Recent studies have concluded there is no time limit for the use of an intrauterine device (I U D, loop). But I U Ds often cause cramping and bleeding, especially when first inserted. There is a very small risk of other complications such as infections, perforation of the uterus, and pregnancy. I U Ds are not known to cause cancer. Why not ask your doctor his reason for wanting to remove the I U D? Because it was inserted in Berkeley?

---

it is medically undesirable that a married couple should procreate. As a means of birth control for social reasons it does not rate as 'treatment' which the NHS must provide. It can however, be arranged either through a general practitioner or, in certain parts of the country, through a FPA clinic. The fee, generally speaking, is not likely to be very high.

Menstruation and Intercourse

I read recently that there is no chance of pregnancy during the menstrual period, especially if a tampon is used. Is this true?

Many women enjoy intercourse most during menstruation; some because they do not fear pregnancy at this time and others because of normal physiological variations in sexual desire. The practice is not known to be harmful.

The chances of pregnancy occurring as a result of intercourse during menstruation are very remote. Tampons cannot be relied upon as contraceptive devices, though some women use them for this purpose. When worn during intercourse they may be irritating to the male member.

(Note: 'Very remote' means that the possibility exists, as it did for the girl who sent the following letter.)

Dear Dr Schoenfeld:
Please don't underestimate the power of conception during menstruation.
When I was 18 I listened to those who said the possibility of getting pregnant during menstruation was slight. The first time my boyfriend and I had intercourse without protection while I had my period – I got pregnant.
The chance might be slight – but the chance to be pregnant is there and then oftimes one has to go through hell to get an abortion.
Please tell the girls to use protection with or without their period.

Thank you

Lost Tampons

Are there any harmful effects from having a tampon caught inside you? Should it be removed by a doctor or is there a simple 'at home' method?

Women are often seen by physicians for this complaint. The cause is usually insertion of a second tampon, thus pushing the first high into the vagina. Another cause may be explained by the preceding letter.

The tampon may actually be forgotten until the lady or a friend notices a foul odour. A vaginal discharge may also be found.

If the patient or a very close friend cannot remove the tampon, a physician can, quickly and without discomfort.

Another common complaint is of a 'lost' tampon. On examination no tampon is found and patient and physician are equally puzzled since it is not possible to force a tampon into the uterus. The probable explanation is that the patient has forgotten she removed the tampon.

Falls and Miscarriages

Two years ago, I had a bad fall during my second month of pregnancy and had a miscarriage two weeks later. Was the fall the cause of this? Since then I have been unable to get pregnant again. Is it true that after a miscarriage it is hard to get pregnant? Will I ever be able to have children? I am 20 years old.

Miscarriages are rarely caused by falls; usually the cause is unknown. A previous miscarriage will not, in itself, cause a decrease in fertility unless there has also been an infection involving the uterus, tubes, or ovaries. You ought to consult a gynaecologist to determine whether there is any physical condition preventing conception.

Abortions

I would appreciate any possible information you could give me regarding the obtaining of an abortion at one and a half months of pregnancy. Great family and financial strain is at stake.

In Colorado, Maryland, and North Carolina, abortions may be legally performed when the life of the mother is threatened or it seems likely that the physical or mental health of the mother would be impaired by continuation of the pregnancy, when there is substantial risk the baby would be seriously deformed or retarded, or when the pregnancy results from rape. California permits abortions for the above reasons (except for the possibility that the baby would have congenital defects) and adds incest as a permissible reason.

For example, if a woman's past history indicated she was a serious suicide risk, an abortion would probably be allowed if so recommended by two psychiatrists. A woman who develops dangerously high blood-pressure when pregnant would also be allowed an abortion if recommended by her physicians. These two examples involve risk to the life of the mother and have been legitimate reasons for abortions even before recent changes in state laws.

More often, however, the issues are not so clear. Hospital abortion committees must decide whether continuation of pregnancy might cause illness but not permanent illness to the mother. A woman who wishes to limit the size of her family or who is unmarried and does not wish to raise a child unaided will not be permitted a legal abortion.

Many women in this position have their babies and give them no less love than if they were married. Others give their babies up for adoption, a solution which has enriched the lives of many couples who would otherwise be childless.

One of the paradoxes of this situation is that those who can best afford (financially) to have a child, may most easily obtain an abortion. Shortly after the Second World War, Japan legalized and encouraged abortions. (The birth rate was cut in half.) Abortions in Japan are performed under sterile conditions by competent practitioners and they are inexpensive ($10–$20). But an airplane ticket there and back costs about $750. And there are other travel expenses, hotels, etc. The total cost is approximately $1,000.

The number of illegal abortions performed on American women each year is unknown. A million is one reasonable guess. I'm blurting out no secret when I say that abortions are major sources of income for Mexican border towns like Tijuana or Juarez. Or that many a trip to Mexico City is not for tourism alone.

Fortunately, most girls who have illegal abortions go through the experience unharmed physically. They may owe much to the body's natural resistance to disease.

But many girls who have an illegal abortion develop a low-grade pelvic infection discovered only weeks afterwards. Just as P I D (pelvic inflammatory disease) resulting from gonorrhea may cause sterility, so may P I D resulting from an abortion done under unsterile conditions.

Girls who have had illegal abortions should be examined afterwards by their own doctors or another gynaecologist. Few practising physicians will find this a new experience.

Some girls die because of illegal abortions. They die from rare reactions to anaesthetics when trained medical personnel are not immediately available. They die of gangrene. They die of tetanus. They die from loss of blood. Each death is an execution by the state.*

*The situation is totally different in the UK. The Abortion Act 1967 made termination of pregnancy a legitimate procedure in the

55

Circumcision

What is the current medical opinion on routine male infant circumcision? Some of our friends tell us doctors now say don't bother unless it's a necessity (e.g., a tight foreskin). But are there other considerations, for or against? All the men in our families were circumcised (routinely, not ritually). Of other men we know, it's about fifty–fifty. We are concerned because we may have a son in a couple of months.

Jews, Arabs, and other tribes circumcise all male infants. The origins of male circumcision were related to sound health practices at the time and later became incorporated into religious rituals. In the Jewish religion, the circumcision ceremony or *briss* is a festive occasion attended by many family members and friends.

United Kingdom (apart from Northern Ireland) in certain specified circumstances. Principal among them is the belief held and certified by two different doctors that the continuance of the pregnancy will involve a greater risk either to the life or to the physical or mental health of the pregnant woman than will its termination. In such a situation – and in one or two others which would be less likely to be relevant to you – it is legitimate for a surgeon to bring the pregnancy to a conclusion quite openly in either a hospital or a nursing home.

Unfortunately, in practical terms the problem is not quite as simple as many people imagine. In the first place it must be appreciated that the decision as to the relative risks of terminating or continuing the pregnancy is one which it is for the doctors, not the pregnant woman, to make. Some doctors hold more rigid views than others on what is in each case essentially a matter of opinion. Again, some gynaecologists are reluctant to do the actual operation, other than in certain very well defined circumstances. Terminations can be and are done in NHS hospital beds, but sometimes this is not practicable, either because of the reluctance of the surgeon attached to a particular hospital to undertake a termination when he is not satisfied of its justification, or because of the delay which may occur before admission from the waiting list is possible.

I remember the *briss* of a second cousin in the Bronx when I was 11 years old. The apartment was crowded with people and laden with meats, fresh-baked pastries, and home-made sweet wine. My mother pointed to a small middle-aged man with a goatee and said, 'That's the *moyle*. He's the same one you had.'

I was thus doubly interested as I watched the *moyle* use a small sharp knife to deftly and swiftly remove the foreskin of my infant cousin. So quickly was it done the baby hardly cried. Immediately there was a chorus of congratulations and everyone set upon the food and wine, all of us getting a little loaded.

In a number of towns there are now various advisory services which will help women who qualify for an abortion under the Act to meet up with a surgeon who will perform it in a nursing home. Some of these centres are, one has to admit, a little suspect and there is no doubt that a few homes and a few doctors have prospered greatly by charging exorbitant fees to people who in their distress have no option but to pay them. There are, however, other schemes whereby an all inclusive charge is made which is not usually beyond the pocket of the woman who is entitled to be aborted, though the raising of it may cause some hardship. Any woman seeking an abortion would be wise to approach her general practitioner in confidence in the first place. If he cannot help her she might try the local FPA clinic, where a sympathetic view will usually be taken.

Termination is desirable before the end of the twelfth week of pregnancy, as it can then be undertaken by the vaginal route and the time required under medical supervision is only 24 or 48 hours. After the twelfth week a different technique is necessary, which involves opening the abdomen and consequently a longer period in hospital. Doctors will not normally undertake a termination after eighteen weeks have elapsed, and many doctors will not do it after sixteen weeks at the outside.

Despite the liberal Act, 'back street' abortionists, unqualified and untrained, still operate. Not only are their activities outside the law, they are extremely dangerous people, who frequently damage their 'patients' for life and not infrequently kill them. Any woman who undergoes a termination at the hands of these people may well be committing suicide in a remarkably unpleasant manner.

There are two methods of infant male circumcision used in hospitals today. One involves the use of a metal bell and circular clamp. The bell is placed over the head of the penis and the foreskin pulled over it. After screwing the clamp tightly against the bell, the foreskin between the two, a scalpel is used to cut away the part of the foreskin covering the bell. The clamp remains closed for a few minutes to prevent bleeding.

A new method uses a plastic bell and twine. The bell is placed over the head of the penis and the foreskin pulled up over it. Then the twine is tied tightly around the bell, the foreskin between the twine and the plastic bell. After a few days the foreskin falls off, its blood supply cut off by the twine.

It is said that the baby feels little pain during this procedure, yet he always cries. How much discomfort, emotional or physical, the baby really experiences neither I nor anyone can tell you. Nor can anyone later recall the first few days of life (though some people claim to have recalled their births on LSD trips).

CURRENT MEDICAL OPINION

Until recently, it was felt that all males should be circumcised. One reason for the practice of universal male circumcision is that, otherwise, daily retraction of the foreskin is required. Foreskin retraction prevents phimosis or tightening of the foreskin and allows cleansing the glans or head of the penis of smegma, a cheesy substance which accumulates under the foreskin.

Several studies have shown that the wives of uncircumcised males are far more likely to get cancer of the cervix than the wives of circumcised males. This increase in cancer of the cervix has been blamed on smegma and circumcision is advanced as a preventive health measure.

Another reason given for circumcision is that diseases such

as syphilis will be noticed more readily in the absence of a foreskin.

But provided there is an elementary knowledge of hygiene and an adequate supply of soap and water there seems to be no absolute reason why circumcision must be practiced. Since physicians are themselves divided on the question of the necessity for circumcision you will not go far wrong whatever your decision.

(An article in *Fact* magazine by a physician who condemned circumcision as a barbaric and unnecessary procedure apparently stirred up unconscious memories in many readers. Here are more letters concerning the great circumcision flap.)

Since your questioner also wanted reasons against routine circumcision, please include this mother's:

1) The foreskin protects a baby's sensitive glans from diaper rash, etc.

2) Circumcised babies sometimes get sores on the urinary opening and try to hold back urine.

3) The inside of the foreskin is erotically sensitive and enables a hip woman to give her man added pleasure in foreplay or fellatio.

A Fresno woman writes:

I wish you had come out more strongly against the cruel practice of circumcision. Or at least that you had mentioned the tragic loss of sensitivity in the glans penis brought on by continual chafing against underclothes and legs. I maintain that circumcision can also contribute to difficulty in sexual arousal as well as a diminished satisfaction in the sex act.

Or simply, to quote a melancholy Jewish friend, ' The only way to lose a foreskin is to wear it off.'

A possible solution is suggested by this letter from San Francisco:

In The Source *Michener refers to cosmetic surgery where one can regain a foreskin. Is this operation still done, and if so, where?*

Mutilated

Another argument for circumcision, besides preventing cancer in women, is that there is only one recorded case of cancer of the penis in a Jew. And it happened that he was uncircumcised.

As for the question of decreased sensitivity of the glans, Masters and Johnson studied this question in their researches into the physiology of sex. Extensive neurological testing of such sensations as touch and pain sensitivity failed to reveal any differences in those with or without foreskins.

The circumcised can once more stand proudly erect, their heads held high.

Vaginal Exercises

I have read that the women of some ancient cultures used combinations of herbs, etc., to temporarily tighten the vagina. If there ever were, in fact, such concoctions, is there anything available to today's women that will bring the same results?

Any medication presently known that can produce this effect is either inadequate for the result desired or harmful or both. Exercises to strengthen the muscles supporting the vagina are your best bet. My well-toned secretary suggests the following medically sound method:

'By pretending there is a finger within the vaginal canal and attempting to hold on to it, you should achieve this tightening. Do this twenty or thirty times each day and you will find that the vaginal canal has lessened in its circumference and that you can tighten and hold at will.'

She says this exercise can be done while washing dishes, waiting for a bus, reading, during coffee breaks, etc. Being uptight isn't always a bummer.

The Beard

Are there any treatments for increasing facial hair on a 23-year-old male? I should like to grow a beard but lack the means. Boy, then I'd get the girls!

If you are otherwise equipped with normal male features, chances are that nothing you can do will make your facial hair denser, except, perhaps, a few more years. To be certain, you could consult an endocrinologist.*

Underarm Hair

Why do girls have to shave under their arms? If they are modelling clothes that's all right but I find a downy, curly armpit a delightful aphrodisiac. Why aren't there more?

Why do you have different standards for models? I'll pass along your observation to a tall, gazelle-like model friend with my own advice that there is no medical reason for shaving axillary (armpit) hair.

Breast Hair

What do men think of hair on women's breasts? Playboy foldouts never have hair – is it distasteful? Don't want to give my name but I'm a self-conscious 16-year-old girl.

*In the UK, such a person should begin by consulting a general practitioner, who will then, if he thinks it desirable, refer him to an endocrinologist.

Undoubtedly many men are turned on by hair on a girl's breasts. Perhaps the editors of *Playboy* believe their readers are turned on by airbrushes. My favourite Israeli topless dancer recommends plucking unwanted breast hair. Ouch!

A Close Shave

For cosmetic reasons and sex appeal, I have been interested for some time in removing my pubic hair. I initially tried scissors which left stubbles; a safety razor leaves red marks and bumps which are both unattractive and painful. An electric razor is better but still unsatisfactory. I called an electrologist who removes hair, but she found my request most peculiar and refused to undertake the work.

Can you suggest a solution to the problem? Is there any reason to believe removal of pubic hair would be either unhealthful or dangerous?

Most Middle Eastern women routinely shave their pubic hair but I leave to you and your chafed friends the question of whether this practice will enhance your sex appeal. It does not seem medically dangerous.

Cautious use of a depilatory or one of the newer electric razors would seem the best solution to your problem. I would advise against permanent removal since you might some day move to a colder climate.

(Note: Judging from the volume of mail received in response to the preceding question and answer, shaving pubic hair is definitely not confined to the Middle East. Excerpts from three letters follow.)

A leading manufacturer of safety razors (Gillette) recently placed on the market something called a ' Scairdy Kit'. The ad dealt with the problem of very brief bathing suits but the letter from the girl who shaves made me wonder. Perhaps she needs instruction in the use of lather or brushless cream.

She will have far better results if she uses an electric hair clipper such as the ones barbers use. The OOOO blade is the finest one and will not leave unsightly stubble, irritate the skin or cause abrasions.

For shaving, use alcohol – it eliminates abrasions and little bumps. This was told to me by a psychiatrist.

Home Deliveries

I am planning to deliver my own baby at home with the help of my husband. I have had two children before (in the hospital) and had no difficulty in pregnancy, labour, or delivery. The question is regarding the hospital 'mysteries' which are performed after the birth – such as drops in the baby's eyes – are they really necessary? If so, could I get them? Is there any book we could read which would prove helpful on the technical side – how to cut the cord, etc.? Oh, and is this illegal?

Almost all babies born in the United States today are delivered in a hospital. There are many reasons for this practice, the most important being the availability of prompt medical attention in cases of emergencies or complications of pregnancy, labour, childbirth, and the post-delivery period.

Some of the disadvantages are cost, leaving your home and family (though many women enjoy this respite from their daily routine), and subjection to certain hospital practices you might find restrictive.

Hospitalization is available for all women, even those with little or no financial resources, though you might not have the hospital or physician of your choice. Many hospitals permit the husband to be present through labour and delivery.

Though your previous two pregnancies were uneventful, you should soon consult a physician. You may feel perfectly well but regular visits to a physician, the frequency increasing as the time of delivery draws near, are necessary, in order to check your blood pressure, urine, growth of the foetus, and foetal heart beat. These measures are important for your health as well as the baby's.

Antibiotic eye drops are used immediately after birth in order to prevent blindness due to gonorrhoeal infection, once an important disease of infants. Because of the prevalence of gonorrhoea today, it is likely infant blindness would once more be a serious problem if antibiotic eyedrops were not used routinely.

It might be illegal to deliberately plan to deliver one's own baby; though this sometimes happens accidentally. While I can certainly appreciate why you and your husband wish to deliver your baby unaided, I must advise against it. What would you do if sudden rapid bleeding occurred? What if the first part of the baby to appear was its shoulder, feet, or rump? No amount of reading could prepare you for these not uncommon eventualities. You must then ask yourself whether the beauty of delivering a baby unaided is worth risking the lives or health of you and your baby.*

*The social and legal situations are rather different in this country. Although the majority of confinements take place in hospitals or in maternity units, there are still quite a number of domiciliary deliveries with the midwife and/or the patient's general practitioner in attendance. Generally speaking, it is desirable for the first baby to be born in hospital and the fourth and any subsequent babies also. In most hospitals husbands are encouraged to be with their wives through the first stage of labour, and in many they are permitted to remain throughout the whole delivery.

The Midwives Act makes it illegal for any man who is not a registered medical practitioner to deliver a woman of her baby other than

Fears Homosexuality

The fact is that I am a homosexual, or almost one. I have had sex with females before, yes, but I am still headed the other way I'm sure. I feel very seriously about this because I do not want to be one. Whatever you say will be appreciated – please, please help.

Most large cities have publicly operated psychiatric clinics which could assist you. Or you might consider private psychiatric care. The medical association in your county will supply you with a list of psychiatrists in your area.*

---

in an emergency. This includes a man's own wife. It also makes it illegal for a woman who is not a registered midwife to act as a midwife unless she does so under the direct supervision of a registered medical practitioner; nurses who are undergoing their training are, of course, not thus restricted.

I share Dr Schoenfeld's view that no one ought to attempt to go through pregnancy and confinement without the supervision of a doctor or a midwife. The principal reason for the fall in maternal and infant mortality has been prevention rather than cure. The mere fact that this woman has gone through two previous pregnancies without difficulty is no guarantee that the next pregnancy may be similarly uneventful. Regular examinations would make it unlikely that any condition would develop to an extent which might prejudice either her health or that of the baby without being recognized at an early stage and appropriate action being taken. The 'mysteries' which are performed after the infant's birth are all of them necessary and all of them aimed at securing the safety and well-being of mother and child; she would be most unwise not to go through the pregnancy routines which have proved to be so valuable.

*I would advise this reader to have a frank and confidential talk with his general practitioner and ask him to arrange for him to see a psychiatrist. If, as is likely, there is little cause for worry, his fears will be put to rest and he will receive any guidance which he may require.

Panty Raider

For the past five years, my son has had the habit of taking panties (from where I don't know) and putting them under his mattress. When he was younger he would put them on over his pyjamas after I left his bedroom. He's cheerful, well adjusted, and seems masculine in every other way. But I am worried about this habit.

Should I speak to him about it or continue to ignore it? Should I take him to a psychologist or psychiatrist?

Your son should have professional help now. In most large communities there are family service agencies which could refer you to someone for assistance. Your local health department and county medical society are also valuable sources for this kind of information.*

Low Blow

Practically every man at some time (or several times) in his life suffers from an accidental blow to his testes. As common as this may be I have never seen a first-aid or medical publication advising how to relieve the distress caused by this mishap. What can be done in case of such an injury?

As you lie writhing on the floor it is helpful to remember that time and/or medication for pain usually suffice to relieve the distress caused by a swift kick.

Occasionally real damage may be done to the testicles, so if you have any doubt seek medical attention immediately.

*The reader does not say how old the son is, but this is a situation in which it would be wise to persuade him to consult his general practitioner who would put him in touch with a specialist should this seem necessary.

66

R.N.'s

Several men who have been bedridden in hospitals have told me that certain ministrations performed on them by a nurse – such as a massage – caused them to have an erection. As described to me, the nurse deals with this problem with something like a judo chop, or flick of the finger which results in detumescence. I would like to know exactly what the nurse has done and how it causes loss of erection. Also, I would appreciate knowing if this action is considered necessary on her part and for what reason. These men told me their reactions ranged from some embarrassment to acute humiliation. What concerns me is that someday I may find myself in the same situation.

Some nurses may likewise be embarrassed by the situation you describe. However, a judo chop or flick of the finger seems an extreme response though it is apparently all too frequent. The detumescence is a reaction to pain and fright, both of which caused blood to leave organs not needed for flight or fight.

Fortunately most nurses would not intentionally do harm to one of their favourite anatomical objects.

Bathroom VD

Dear Dr Schoenfeld:
My date sometimes takes me to bars and nightclubs in the rougher parts of our town.

Can you tell me if it's possible to get a venereal disease in the bathroom?

Yours truly,
Phyllis M—

Certainly it's possible to get a venereal disease in the bathroom. But bathroom floors are usually very cold and hard.

In other words, only in the rarest of circumstances could a person contract a venereal disease other than by intimate physical contact.

Boyfriend Has Gonorrhoea

My boyfriend had a discharge from his penis, saw a doctor, and was treated for gonorrhoea. I haven't noticed any symptoms in myself. Is it necessary that I get a check-up? If so, where can I go? I have very little money and no regular doctor.

Gonorrhoea in the male usually makes itself known by a discharge from the penis, itching, and burning on urination. In the female, however, there may be less obvious symptoms or no symptoms at all. If your boyfriend had gonorrhoea (and I assume you two are friendly) there is a good chance you may have it also, even though you may feel perfectly well. Most cities of any size operate clinics where you may receive treatment of venereal diseases free of charge. If you are a college student you may go to your student health service.*

Vietnam VD

I have read a few newspaper articles referring to the high incidence of VD among American servicemen in Vietnam. My boyfriend is due to return from Vietnam in about three weeks, at which time he will be discharged from active duty.

*There should be no difficulty in finding a venereal diseases clinic – often they are referred to euphemistically as 'special' clinics – at a near-by general hospital. Also public lavatories in large towns usually display a poster giving details of such clinics. Alternatively the family doctor should be consulted or, if the reader were a college student, the doctor in charge of student health. Wherever a person in this condition goes for help and advice, complete confidentiality can be guaranteed.

How can I be sure that he is free of VD before we have relations, without insulting him, in an effort to protect myself?

The high incidence of VD among servicemen in Vietnam is due mainly to gonorrhoea. Your boyfriend will probably be returning by ship, a trip of two weeks or so. In this time the symptoms of gonorrhoea would become known and he would be treated by the doctors on the ship.

Returning GIs and their doctors are quite familiar with the Vietnam VD problem. Sometimes, the type of gonorrhoea found in Vietnam is difficult to treat with penicillin alone but, so far, alternate drugs have been effective. If your boyfriend should notice a discharge from his penis or pain when he urinates, both of you should be seen by a physician.

Syphilis is a more complicated disease. Its first stage is a chancre, or painless ulcer, appearing on the penis, vulva, in the vagina, mouth, rectum, on the finger, or any other place where sexual contact has been made.

Untreated, the chancre will disappear but more serious stages of the disease follow. Blood tests show the presence of syphilis thirty to ninety days after the initial sexual contact.

If venereal diseases were not associated with shame and guilt, they could soon be virtually eliminated from our society. Those who suspect they may have a communicable disease should promptly seek medical attention and urge their friends to do the same. The prevention and treatment of disease is an act of love.

Female Gonorrhoea

If gonorrhoea in the female is often without symptoms, is it also without harm to her – except as a social stigma?

Though symptoms in the female may be minimal or even

absent, gonorrhoea often spreads from the vagina and urethra to cause an infection of the cervix, uterus, Fallopian tubes, and ovaries. Such a condition is called pelvic inflammatory disease or P I D and gonorrhoea is the chief cause of P I D.

P I D causes fever, pain in the lower abdomen, and is an important cause of sterility due to the inflammation and subsequent scarring of the Fallopian tubes.

Another complication of gonorrhoea, found in both males and females, is a type of arthritis. But this is an uncommon finding.

These complications are further reasons for seeking medical attention whenever gonorrhoea is suspected.

Treatment usually consists of two shots of penicillin, though with more and more strains of the gonococcus becoming resistant to penicillin, alternate antibiotics may be required.

In order to control the spread of the disease and to prevent reinfection, both (or all) parties involved must receive adequate diagnosis and treatment. That's the reason you may be questioned by a V D investigator at your local V D clinic. He's not just nosy, nor does he fink to the police.

Here's a little poem on the subject by Richard Brautigan:

> *Flowers for Those You Love*
>
> Butcher, baker, candlestick maker,
> anybody can get V D,
> including those you love.
>
> Please see a doctor
> if you think you've got it.
>
> You'll feel better afterwards
> and so will those you love.

Mathematics

Does promiscuity increase the risk of contracting a venereal disease?

If venereal diseases are present in a community, increasing one's sexual contacts also increases the risk of contracting one of these diseases. Venereal diseases, especially gonorrhoea and syphilis, are present in large communities in epidemic proportions. Treatment of V D used to be a simple matter but recently many penicillin-resistant bacteria have appeared and alternate drugs must often be employed. The risk of contracting a venereal disease increases directly with the number of one's partners. At the first suspicion of V D you should contact your physician or local health department. Help keep your community safe for love!

Types of VD

Are there more venereal diseases besides gonorrhoea and syphilis?

The diseases usually classified as venereal are gonorrhoea, syphilis, chancroid, granuloma inguinale, and lymphogranuloma venereum. The last three are fortunately rare and usually found only in sailors and other visitors to exotic ports.

V D is unpleasant and may be dangerous if untreated – but it's better to have had a positive Wassermann test than never to have loved at all.

VD and Penicillin

I have been told there is a penicillin tablet available by prescription which can be taken thirty minutes before intercourse and thirty minutes after which will effectively prevent venereal infection. What do you think of such a programme?

Not much. As you suggest, most venereal infections could be prevented by the prophylactic or preventive use of penicillin.

But such a programme would do far more harm than good for the following reasons:

1) Bacteria such as those which cause gonorrhoea are becoming more resistant to penicillin therapy. If everyone dropped a penicillin tablet each time he had sex, it would only be a matter of time before the drug was totally ineffective for treating V D. There is a growing fear among public-health specialists that this may happen in the foreseeable future anyway.

2) The more one is exposed to a drug like penicillin, the greater one's chances of developing an allergy to it, and many people are sensitive to penicillin already. The chances of dying from a penicillin reaction are greater than from a venereal disease.

Vaccines against VD?

Is there any reason (biological, not sociological) why vaccines have not been developed for use against the venereal diseases? The micro-organisms causing them are known, are they not?

Developing vaccines against the major venereal diseases, gonorrhoea and syphilis, presents problems aside from 'moral' barriers certain to be raised by church groups. Gonorrhoea is a disease which does not give the gift of future immunity. The most feasible type of vaccine would be similar to cholera vaccinations which must be renewed every six months.

Research continues on a vaccine for syphilis with promising, but so far, unsuccessful results. One very important factor to be considered is the necessity to have the vaccine not give false positive blood tests for syphilis.

A vaccine which caused positive blood tests for syphilis would do more harm than good since it would be impossible to differentiate between those who had the disease and required treatment and those who had only been vaccinated against it.

At present the VDRL, Wassermann, or similar blood tests are the best diagnostic tools we have for detecting syphilis in its later stages.

Acne and Sex

Somebody told me that the cause of adolescent acne is lack of sex, but I engage in sexual relations at least once and often two or three times a week and I still have acne. What's a girl to do?

Perhaps this very common belief arose because acne is often associated with adolescence, a time when great interest in sex is usually unmatched by actual deeds. Lack of sex is not the cause of acne nor is sex a cure. Most people with acne are helped by exposure to sunlight, frequent washing with soap and water, and proper diet. Your own doctor can best advise individual treatment.

Vaginal Yeast Infections

I had a vaginal discharge and terrible itching so I saw my doctor. He told me I had a yeast infection and prescribed vaginal suppositories.

What is a yeast infection? is it necessarily caused by sex? is it contagious (like I have a boyfriend and all)?

Next to Trichomonas vaginalis, yeast (monilia, fungus) is the chief cause of vaginal infections. The same organism (monilia albicans) causes 'thrush' in the mouths of children. In fact, an important cause of thrush in children is transmission from the mother during childbirth.

Yeast is often present in the vagina without causing any symptoms. But when broad spectrum antibiotics are given (tetracycline, for example), normal vaginal bacteria are killed, thus allowing the yeast organisms to grow and multiply. Diabetic women are especially susceptible to monilial infections.

Symptoms of monilial infections are a vaginal discharge, irritation of the vulvae (lips of the vagina), and itching.

The same symptoms may be caused by other infections, such as trichomonas or, less commonly, gonorrhoea. That's another reason for seeing a doctor whenever these symptoms occur. I've known girls who borrow medication from girlfriends because they think they have the same disease. But a pelvic and microscopic examination is necessary, for often there are 'mixed' vaginal infections.

Treatment includes application of gentian violet (which accounts for many purple bottoms) or vaginal suppositories.

Monilial infections are not transmitted by sexual contact but tend to recur, so don't be discouraged if more treatments are necessary.

Vaginal Trichomonas Infections

Can one become infected with vaginal trichomonas through digital anal penetration and subsequent digital vaginal penetration? My gynaecologist noted that the microbe is normally found in parts of the digestive system.

Trichomonas vaginalis is a single-celled organism which is readily identified under a microscope by its tail, or flagella, and peculiar, rapid movement. The trichomonad found in the digestive tract, Trichomonas hominis, is identical in appearance and the two are distinguished only by their location in the body. Since twenty per cent of all women have Trichomonas vaginalis organisms, it seems likely that the two are, in fact, the same.

Vaginitis caused by trichomonas is characterized by itching

and a foul smelling yellow-green discharge. In the male there are usually no symptoms though there may be a thin discharge and some burning or itching on urination. Rarely, the infection may descend to the testicles. The presence of trichomonads does not necessarily mean that there is also an infection present. As indicated above, they are normally found in the digestive tract and may be found in the vagina even when there are no symptoms.

Trichomonads are usually transmitted from one person to another through sexual contact. The means that you suggest is certainly plausible if T. vaginalis and T. hominis are really the same critters. And it is another reason women should use toilet tissue front to back rather than back to front.

Treatment of Trichomonas vaginalis vaginitis has become simple in recent years; pills are taken by mouth for ten days. Both male and female must take the medication or the infection will bounce back and forth like a ping-pong ball.

Itch for Information

Dear Dr Schoenfeld:
I've had two recent attacks of crabs – in my eyelashes! No one seems to know too much about the various types of crab-attacks.

I had crabs in one eyelash – rid myself of them (I thought) – and three weeks later I found myself infested again – in the same eyelash.

Are there different types of crabs? Why do I only get them in my eyelash? What methods of transmission are there? And what's the best way to get them out of my eyelash? So they won't come back?

Thank you
Jennifer —

While scratching my crotch I am writing to ask what to do about crabs. I've tried alcohol and soap and water without success. Some very close friends have the same problem.

Crabs or crab lice are spread by intimate physical contact or sharing infested bedding. There are three types of crab lice: Pediculus capitis (head lice), Pediculus corporis (body lice), and Pediculus pubis (pubic lice).

The lice attach themselves to the skin and lay their eggs on the body hairs close to the skin (except for P. corporis or body lice which lay their eggs in clothing). They have the appearance of minute crabs and are nourished by the blood of the host.

A nude beach devotee has suggested placing sand in the affected areas on the assumption that the crabs will then stone themselves to death with the sand granules. If this is ineffective there are several preparations you can purchase without a prescription at your pharmacy. One is Cuprex, which is in a kerosene-like base; another is Topicide.*

The treatment is simple. Rub the liquid into the affected areas (don't get it in your eyes!), wait half an hour to an hour, and shower or bathe. Then comb out the hair with a fine-toothed comb. Most important also is laundering or dry-cleaning bed sheets and garments at the same time treatment is started. Rarely, a second treatment is necessary. Don't use D D T powder alone since this will only kill the crab lice but not their eggs. Your very close friends should also be treated or you'll be reinfected.

Why crabs in the eyelashes? Depend's on one's point of view.

*In this country Ascabiol, Esoderm or Lorexane are available without prescription.

76

Tongue in Cheek?

Can infectious hepatitis be contracted through cunnilingus?

This is an excellent way – if the recipient of your affection has the disease.

Frost-a-Lung

The 1–15 October 1967 issue of the East Village Other *ran a letter for a new turn-on. In case you haven't seen the letter, it says to buy a can of 'instant icer', 'frost-a-glass' or a similar glass chiller, spray some in a plastic bag, allow to warm up and inhale. Could you please tell us if this is harmful?*

Glass chillers use Freon gases to cause an icing effect. When inhaled, these gases apparently produce a high, but may also cause severe lung irritation.

Several deaths have resulted from inhaling gas directly from the aerosol container. These deaths were probably due to freezing and subsequent swelling of the larynx. The air passage to the larynx is cut off and the victim dies a horrible death by strangulation. Using a plastic bag eliminates the danger of instant death but the gas is still irritating to the lungs. This is an example of a perfectly legal but very dangerous way to turn on.

Impatient

I am in the hospital with hepatitis, am doing well, and will be released soon. My doctor says I can't drink for a year but what I really care about is can I drop pills (stimulants), take acid, and smoke marijuana. How long do I have to wait before I can do these things again?

Your own doctor is more familiar with your medical history and you should ask him these questions. If you are reluctant to do so, ask one of the house officers.

Hepatitis

Two of my room-mates are in the hospital with hepatitis. Their doctor says they have serum hepatitis. Is there more than one type? Could I have caught it from them?

There are two types of viral hepatitis; serum and infectious. Infectious hepatitis is thought to be spread by faecal, or rarely, urinary contamination. Recently, an outbreak of hepatitis at San Quentin Prison was traced to a pissed-off inmate urinating in a huge soup pot.

Your roommates, however, have the type spread through contaminated blood. Users of narcotics and amphetamines who share inadequately sterilized needles and syringes have a very high rate of hepatitis. Hepatitis is a most disabling and often fatal disease and I would guess that those who use needles for their highs become ill or die more often from contaminated needles or syringes than from overdoses of drugs.

Symptoms of viral hepatitis are dark-coloured urine, light-coloured stools, fatigue, and jaundice or yellowing of the skin and eyes.

The incubation period of viral hepatitis is so long (up to six months) that many people can contract the disease before symptoms appear in any of them.

MACE and Tear Gas

What's the best amateur first-aid for persons who have just been tear gassed or MACED?

Both tear gas and MACE cause irritation to the eyes, skin, and nasal passages. Concentrated doses when inhaled may produce pulmonary oedema or an accumulation of fluid in the lungs.

The best first-aid treatment is to run large amounts of cool tap water over the affected areas, including the eyes. Oxygen may be necessary if tear gas is inhaled.

Launder clothes or drapes which have been saturated with tear gas.

Doggone Good

Dear Dr Schoenfeld:
Do you know of any way to eat cheaply and still get a good balanced diet? Is it all right to eat dog food? What else is available?

Sincerely,
Bernard —

Dear Bernard:
The Department of Nutrition of your local health department has information about inexpensive balanced diets.

I don't believe canned dog food meets health standards for human consumption. Many children eat dry dog biscuits without apparent harm but also without much benefit.

I hope a lack of abundant financial resources does not force you to go to the dogs.

Sincerely,
Eugene Schoenfeld, M.D.

Hair Raising

I hear tell that bull sperm does wonders. It makes one's hair grow extremely fast and can be obtained somewhere in Mexico.

Could you confirm this? If so, could you give me a few addresses where it can be purchased? Please hurry with answer, if possible.

Bull sperm does wonders for cows but not for men. I know of no evidence that bull sperm causes hair to grow faster or that it affects hair at all.

But you may be interested in knowing how bull semen is obtained – in case you should encounter a friendly animal.

A cow in heat is placed in a small stall, her private parts facing the bull who is pawing the ground and peering through a barricade. At least two men are needed for the delicate man-oeuvring which follows.

The bull is allowed closer to the cow. As he mounts, one of the men seizes the bull's penis and directs it not to its intended object but off to one side, into a lined collecting bottle. Bulls have gigantic genitals but we might think them poor lovers. One thrust and it's over.

The collected semen is frozen. One ejaculate is then used to artificially inseminate many cows.

Modern sex for cattle seems a drag. And that's no bull.

Immodest Proposal

Can long-continued use of spray deodorants cause cancer of the armpit?

At first, I thought your letter was a put-on. In fact, that might have been your intention, but, nevertheless, you raise an interesting question. Certainly there has been no epidemic of cancer of the axilla or armpit. But spray deodorants have not been in use for very long. Cigarette smoking causes cancer of the lungs but it takes about twenty years to develop. We don't yet have twenty years' experience with spray deodorants.

If it is a major concern in your life, I suggest that daily bathing obviates the need for deodorants. Spray deodorants are an invention largely of Madison Avenue but daily bathing is not. In Africa, for example, those who live near rivers and lakes go to the water's edge at dusk each day to scrub themselves and watch the sunset.

Communal bathing is an event very different from our solitary bath or shower. The Romans knew all about that and the Japanese enjoy it today. (Perhaps people sing in the shower to give the illusion of company.) If you have a large bath tub or shower, consider inviting a friend to join you. Screen out those undesirables who have infectious hepatitis (which possibly could be transmitted in a bath tub), or, more commonly, those who might bitch about the water being either too hot or too cold.

Lugosi's Legions

Does continued donation of blood over a period of years at three-month intervals lead to any harmful physical effects in normal people?

Periodic donation of blood at prescribed intervals has not been known to cause any harmful effects in normal individuals. An interviewer asks the prospective donor a series of questions in order to rule out any medical conditions which might prove harmful to donor or recipient, e.g., hepatitis, malaria, or heart disease.

The donor's blood is then tested for anaemia by taking a few drops of blood from the earlobe or finger. His temperature, pulse, and blood-pressure are checked before blood is actually withdrawn from the arm.

Doctors and nurses at blood banks draw blood quickly and with a minimum of discomfort. As a matter of fact, many of them wear long black capes, shun sunlight, and travel frequently to Transylvania.

Mind and Matter

Do laxatives have any real physical effect or are they just 'mind' pills?

Although constipation may have its origin in psychic processes, laxatives act physically by stimulating the gastrointestinal tract, by increasing the bulk of the stools, or by causing them to be more 'oily' and allowing these 'ruins of meals' to pass more quickly out of the body and into the rest of the universe.

Boom or Bust

Although this problem may seem rather humorous to some, it has finally ceased to be so with myself. When growing up I used to delight in farting a great deal. The louder the funnier, the more offensive the more successful (fartwise). In the army they called me 'big fart'. This used to be a real gas but I think I now am seeing the results of being a 'big fart'. That is, I don't have many friends.

My wife tells me I should stop letting farts, which I have tried to do. She says if I hold them back they will disappear. I just can't hold them back – I feel like I'll bust.

Could you tell me if farts are physical or psychological? Can I hold them back until they disappear, or must I just go on losing friends? By the way, my office-mate put in for another office the other day stating she would like a place with better ventilation. That really hurt.

How does one get rid of, if one does get rid of, farts? Woe is me!

Flatus is the medical term for gas expelled from the rectum. Passing flatus in public is often a hostile act, according to most psychiatrists, a conclusion in which the victims may concur, though the perpetrator may not be consciously aware of this hostility.

AIR SWALLOWING

Flatulence, or gas in the intestinal system, is due to swallowed air and gas produced by certain foods.

People suffering from anxiety often sigh and breathe deeply, thus swallowing large quantities of air. Deformities of the nose and nasal passages or large spaces between teeth may also cause one to swallow large amounts of air

One of the most common causes of flatulence is the habit of chewing gum. Also to be avoided is eating while under emotional strain or eating too rapidly.

DIET

Consuming large amounts of food or swallowing large quantities of liquids with meals will tend towards flatulence. In general, a person who considers this a problem should eat bland, high protein, low fat, low carbohydrate foods.

Avoid gas-producing foods such as cabbage, tomatoes, beans, sugar in large quantities or in concentrated forms (such as candy), fried foods, nuts, raisins, berries or other seedy fruits, spices, licorice (a great sacrifice, I know), alcohol, and carbonated beverages.

Your physician may wish to use a drug to reduce salivary flow since air swallowing accompanies the excessive flow and swallowing of saliva. Excessive salivation often accompanies anxiety, so tranquillizers may be indicated.

Flatus contains large quantities of methane gas, the same gas found in household use. A pretty little laboratory technician once told me she amused herself and her friends by igniting the gas as it was expelled. This amusement is not uncommon. Though I have never heard of harm resulting from this practice, it would seem to represent a fire hazard.

Rumour has it that militant demonstrators plan to employ this weapon to counteract police flame-throwers.

Fast High

Dear Dr Schoenfeld:
My room-mate and I fast regularly, for non-meditational purposes. We have noticed that our minds are sharper and our perceptions keener during our periods of fasting but we didn't know we were getting 'high' as fasting is said to cause.

Could you comment further on this?

Thank you,
Jeanne C—

Dear Jeanne:
People undergoing starvation frequently have hallucinations and other perceptual changes. Certain diets, including the more rigorous macrobiotic schedules, cause the dieter to be in a state of semi-starvation. They walk about 'stoned' all of the time but at the price of being near the borderline of malnutrition.

The cause is unknown but somehow is related to less (or different) nutrient material reaching brain cells.

Sincerely,
Eugene Schoenfeld, M.D.

Macrobiotics

Would you comment on the efficacy of the macrobiotic diet? Are there studies of the diet by people other than macrobiotic disciples?

Georges Osawa in *The Philosophy of Oriental Medicine* states, 'and we shall demonstrate the macrobiotic preparation of delicious and aesthetic meals that cure all illnesses (present or future) giving at the same time longevity and youthfulness to everybody, at no expense and with no special training'.

An article in the 13 March 1967 *Journal of the American Medical Association* reported the case of a 36-year-old woman who was found near death from the effects of diet number seven, the strictest and 'purest' diet in the macrobiotic system. She became interested in macrobiotics in the spring of 1964 and gradually eliminated milk and meat from her diet. In October, her menstrual periods ceased. By November 1964, her diet was limited to brown rice, pressure-cooked or boiled, salted and sprinkled with sesame seeds. She also ate some ground oatmeal, cornmeal, buckwheat, and bread made from cooked rice. Her maximum liquid intake was twelve ounces per day in the form of soup or tea, never water. She remained on this diet until her admission to the hospital eight months later.

Some of the symptoms which developed were weakness, fatigue, weight loss of thirty-five pounds, purple and brown spots on her body and face, swellings on the joints, painful bleeding gums, and a greenish vaginal discharge.

Her symptoms were due solely to malnutrition, especially scurvy, a disease of ascorbic acid or Vitamin C deficiency, the prevention and cure of which was known in the sixteenth century.

Many fad diets are of no apparent physiological harm and may even contribute to good health, but the most rigid of the macrobiotic diets appear to be dangerous. Several deaths have been reported resulting from their use.

Starvation commonly produces a delirious condition, including hallucinations. The ecstatic state reported by many who follow macrobiotic and similar diets may have a simple explanation.

The Sound of Music

I went to a rock dance for the first time last week with my son and daughter. Whether or not the music was good I couldn't say, but the noise was almost deafening. Could loud music harm the ears? I half-jokingly told my children they should wear ear muffs like airport personnel.

An article in the November 1967 *California Medicine* claims that rock bands may be amplifying their music to levels harmful to the ears. The authors measured sound at two auditoriums in the San Francisco Bay Area. They said, 'We believe that we have demonstrated the noise levels produced by some live rock-and-roll bands with the aid of high amplification unmistakably exceed those considered safe for prolonged exposure.'

The risks of high noise levels are greater to performers than to the audience. Impairing hearing may prove to be an occupational hazard of rock bands. Do you hear that, Sam? DO YOU HEAR THAT?

Black Light

Are there any dangers from ultra-violet light? I've got a lot of posters up in my room and am thinking of getting a black light. Does it need a special extension or can it be plugged into a wall socket?

Two types of ultra-violet lamps are commonly available. One is the sun or heat lamp used to maintain golden tans during the winter months, the other is the so-called 'black light' used by prospectors, rock establishments, and physicians.

Sun lamps must be used with caution lest they cause painful

burns to the eyes and skin of the face. Falling asleep under a sun lamp, for instance, could be a serious mistake.

'Black light' is not a health hazard when used with reasonable caution. Thanks to the Contra Costa County (where Orinda is located) Health Department and the Bureau of Occupational Health of the California State Health Department, I have learned that black lights are of no known danger to health so long as they are more than thirty-two inches away from the eyes. Prolonged exposure at a closer distance may cause conjunctivitis or pink eye.

Black lights may be plugged into ordinary wall sockets.

Minimum Requirement

Can you get high with a lot of thiamine hydrochloride (Vitamin B[1])?

I can't. But if I tried I'd get a lot of intestinal irritation and diarrhoea. Smoke one of the underground newspapers instead.

Vitamins and Colds

Do vitamins actually do any good or is that just another 'sell' to the gullible public? If 30 milligrams of Vitamin C is the daily requirement, why do vitamins contain 100 or 250 mg.? How can I get rid of this dependency on a synthesized product like a vitamin and yet not get colds?

Normal people who eat nutritionally adequate diets fool themselves and enrich charlatans if they also take vitamins. Moreover, vitamins may be harmful in large doses.

There is *no* evidence that large doses of Vitamin C or other vitamins prevent colds – otherwise every doctor would advise their use.

The best way known to prevent colds is to eat well, sleep seven to eight hours a night, and exercise regularly.

Hydrangeas

I've heard that hydrangeas are supposed to produce a psychedelic effect stronger than pot. Is there any truth to this?

I've heard the same. But the component of hydrangeas causing the high is probably cyanide. You might get so high you'd never come back.

Belladonna

Some of my friends have taken Asthmadore in large quantities and have become blithering idiots for periods of four to six hours. How dangerous is this? If belladonna is the active ingredient and a speed, why the hallucinations?

Asthmadore is an older preparation used in the treatment of asthma. The active ingredient is belladonna, a drug deriving its name from the women of medieval Italy who took the drug to dilate the pupils of their eyes. 'Bella donnas' were perhaps a little stoned as well. Besides dilated pupils, belladonna causes a dry mouth, rapid heart beat, and difficulty in urination. Doses large enough to cause hallucinations may be dangerous to life. Its effects, especially blurred vision, may last several days. Belladonna is closely related to scopolamine, the active ingredient in sleeping-pill preparations. Neither are 'speeds' (amphetamines) though some of their actions on the body are similar.

Scopolamine

I read about a man who experienced a strange trip by taking twenty-five sleep-inducing tablets. He said that someone (I forget the name) recommended sixteen tablets. I thought that people could kill themselves by taking more than a few sleeping tablets. I was thinking of trying this trip.

If a report were printed that cow plop caused one to be high there would be some who would try it. The letter you refer to caused a reader in Boston to try this trip. Here is a portion of her letter:

I read about this in the letters-to-the-editor column of the East Village Other *and tried it. A highly curious experience but I have an idea that it's fortunate I threw up half an hour after I took them. It took me a day before I could see properly afterward.*

One of the ingredients of certain sleeping pills is scopolamine, a drug similar to belladonna. The first report of poisoning due to belladonna-like compounds in North America dates back to 1676 and was due to tea made from Jimson-weedseeds. The effects of ingesting large quantities of scopolamine are as follows: dry mouth with a sensation of burning, thirst, blurred vision and sensitivity of the eyes to light. The skin is hot, dry, and flushed. A rash may appear over the face, neck, and upper part of the trunk. There may be a sharp rise in body temperature. Blood-pressure rises and heart palpitations may be noted. There may exist simultaneously an urge to urinate and difficulty doing so. The patient is restless, excited, confused, weak, giddy and has muscular incoordination. Nausea and vomiting may occur. Memory is disturbed and there may be confusion about time and place. Hallucinations, especially visual, are common. The effects often last forty-eight hours or longer.

With large doses the blood-pressure drops and breathing becomes more difficult. Death due to respiratory failure occurs after a period of paralysis and coma.

Barbiturates

Recently I've come into many friends who have used yellow jackets but none of them agree or have similar experiences. What kind of high do they produce and how (if at all) harmful are they?

'Yellow jackets' are capsules containing phenobarbital or secobarbital, both barbiturates. The medical uses for barbiturates in this form are for sedation and to induce sleep.

Before the widespread use of marijuana and L S D, barbiturates were commonly used, often in combination with amphetamines or alcohol, to produce a 'high', though 'low' would better describe the experience.

Barbiturates are physically addicting, and once hooked the 'yellow jacket' addict must have his drug every day. Without it he will have withdrawal symptoms worse than those felt by morphine or heroin addicts when they try to kick their habits.

Twenty-four hours after barbiturates are withdrawn from an addict, he experiences twitching of the muscles and uncontrolable shaking of the arms and legs. During the second day, most addicts have one or more *gran mal* convulsions. Between the third and seventh day a psychotic episode begins, marked by vivid hallucinations and delusions.

The 'cold turkey' withdrawal method used for narcotic addicts must not be used for barbiturate addiction. Withdrawal from barbiturates should be carried out in a hospital under strict medical supervision.

Kill Speed

Tell us about 'speed'. What happens to the body and brain when 'meth' (crystals and tabs) is taken in small and large doses?

'Meth' (methamphetamine) is used in medicine for appetite control, mood elevation, and to raise blood pressure when indicated. The drug is usually ingested in five-milligram tablets one to three times a day. Medical reasons for injecting methamphetamine are specific and few.

Tolerance to the amphetamines develops rapidly and increasingly large amounts must be used to achieve the same results. When large amounts are used, blood-pressure may be raised sufficiently high to blow out a blood vessel in the brain, thus causing a stroke.

True addiction, as well, seems to occur. Recently, a patient in a drug-abuse clinic stated that it was harder for him to kick the 'meth' habit than it was to get off heroin. At the time he was shooting up two hundred milligrams of 'crystals' every two hours. He was found dead a few weeks later, apparently from an overdose.

An 18-year-old boy on methamphetamine climbed out of a third-storey window in Berkeley not long ago. He is now confined to a neurological institute, completely paralysed from the effects of a broken back.

Both general and student hospitals are seeing increasingly greater numbers of 16-to-25-year-old people who have caught hepatitis from a needle used to inject methamphetamine. Neither boiling water nor soaking in alcohol will necessarily kill the hepatitis virus found in too many spikes.

Speed kills.

Speed and Pregnancy

I am seven-and-a-half-months pregnant and I sleep twelve hours a day, sometimes more. I take thyroid tablets, but I still seem to lack energy and gain weight fast. Would it be unwise for me to take diet pills? Also, what is 'speed' and what is 'meth'?

A large weight gain during pregnancy may be harmful to you and your unborn baby. Your physician can best advise you about ways to control your diet. 'Speed' is slang for the amphetamines which include dextroamphetamine (Dexedrine), methamphetamine (Methedrine), and amphetamine (Benzedrine). All these drugs have a useful place in medical practice but may be harmful when misused. You would be risking the health of you and your baby by taking 'speed' or other drugs during pregnancy without the advice of your physician.

Speeding the Foetus

What are the effects of Dexedrine, Benzedrine, and 'speed' in general on an unborn child?

As you might imagine, no one has taken two groups of women and given amphetamines to one group and placebos to the other just to determine the effects on unborn children. The effects are probably the same as in adults, i.e., increased heart rate and blood-pressure (the effects on the brain of a foetus are unknown). Since drugs taken during pregnancy may cause congenital defects or endanger the pregnancy itself, my advice is to forego 'speed' lest it adversely affect your child.

Glue Sniffing

Capt. Hippocrates:
A friend of mine has been sniffing glue for many years. He and his rag are inseparable. Lately he just buys toluene by the gallon instead of glue. All the people I know that sniff glue seem to really dig it and so far I've noticed no harmful after-effects. Is the propaganda against glue really true or is it just a good cheap high?

When I was gluing model aeroplanes, we though it a great kick to squeeze out ten-foot-long strips of glue, put a match to them and watch the fire race along the fuse-like glue strips.

Like the mind-affecting properties of L S D, the use of aeroplane glue to get high must have been discovered accidentally, perhaps by a pre-teen innocently working on his models in a poorly ventilated garage. No one really knows the prevalence of glue sniffing but police records show thousands of arrests yearly in some large cities.

The behavioural effects of glue sniffing are usually described as imitating those of alcohol intoxication though there are reports of hallucinations and body–image distortions.

At least ten deaths by suffocation have resulted from the practice of sniffing glue from a plastic sack. Direct toxic effects have included two deaths in young adult males, both of whom had also been drinking alcohol; one, in addition, had a history of sniffing gasoline.

The pharmacology of aeroplane glue is poorly known but many other commercial products can produce similar effects. Examples are lacquers, enamels, paint thinners, paint and varnish removers, brake and lighter fluids, and plastic cements.

The wide variety and easy availability of these products indicate the futility of attempting to curb the use of aeroplane glue for highs by restricting its sale, e.g., statutes in certain municipalities which require mandatory inclusion of a model with each tube of glue sold.

Sniffing glue or other volatile substances may cause kidney or liver damage. It's a bum trip.

Beverage or Drug?

I understand there are millions of people so psychologically dependent on the drug caffeine that they feel they cannot function without strong doses when they wake up.

Most large cities have establishments where extra-strong doses of this drug can be obtained at will. They are shamelessly called 'coffeehouses'.

There sit hour after hour, day after day, many erstwhile useful citizens, lost to society.

Enclosed is a clipping from the 11 December 1967 San Francisco Chronicle. *The article indicates that caffeine may damage cell chromosomes and cause miscarriages. Could you comment, please?*

A German geneticist, Dr Wolfram Ostertag, recently reported that caffeine in coffee and soft drinks may cause miscarriages, birth defects, and changes in cell chromosomes.

His report to a meeting on human genetics at the University of Chicago indicated that in experiments with human cells, the addition of caffeine broke up cell chromosomes.

Caffeine may also affect birth rates. When mice were fed caffeine, the birth rate dropped from the usual five to seven per litter to one or two per litter.

Dr Ostertag said, 'The possibility exists that caffeine is one of the most dangerous mutation-causing agents in man since it is known that caffeine penetrates to the human germinal tissue and through the placental barrier to the human foetus.'

Caffeine is a central nervous stimulant which in small doses produces alertness, wakefulness, talkativeness, and increased urination. Excessive doses cause insomnia and agitation. The drug is commonly used to stimulate comatose patients.

There is increasing evidence that other common drugs, such as aspirin, cause the same changes in cell chromosomes as has been claimed for LSD. The significance of these changes, if they occur, is unknown.

Perhaps coffee will be an illegal drug someday, denounced in State of the Union messages. But one suspects many would continue to use the drug, despite heavy penalties. Coffee beans would be smuggled into the country from near-by Latin American countries to poison the minds and bodies of our youth. But detecting users might be easy, especially in the morning. And that characteristic smell of brewing coffee.

Turning a New Leaf

I have been getting a rather weird high by smoking a tobacco cigarette like a joint. A drag will start me up and two cigarettes will get me totally zonked. I usually don't smoke (except grass). Do you have any ideas about the medical ramifications of this habit?

Cigarettes are a known health hazard. Do you get them from the 'Friendly Stranger'?

8 Out of 10 Doctors . . .

Can you give us some straight information about cigarette smoking? Do you think the habit is really harmful?

I think there is little doubt that cigarette smoking causes lung cancer, emphysema, and perhaps heart disease.

Since the U S Surgeon General's report on the association between cigarette smoking and lung cancer, 85,000 M Ds have given up smoking. Today, only 21 per cent of all M Ds smoke cigarettes and only 16 per cent of those under the age of 35.

The tobacco interests spend more on advertising than any other industry. They are very successfully selling death.

Mickey Finns

I have seen countless old films in which Oriental bartenders slip their unsuspecting customers a 'Mickey Finn' which invariably flashes them out of their skulls in about thirty seconds.

Is there any such drug that, taken orally, would put a person out in less than a minute?

Two types of 'Mickey Finns' were allegedly used. One was chloral hydrate, a sleeping preparation, which induces sleep after twenty or thirty minutes. Like barbiturates, it is especially powerful when given with alcohol.

Another 'Mickey' favoured by bartenders was a strong laxative, a favourite method for getting rid of undesired customers. But only in Hollywood do 'Mickeys' work within one minute.

The Most Dangerous Drug

For several years (I am 31), it has been my custom to have five or six drinks before dinner and two or three after. This drinking does not in any way interfere with my life and I find it enjoyable.

However, I am somewhat concerned about the possibilities of long-term physiological damage. Is it known, for example, that consumption of alcohol at such a rate will cause cirrhosis of the liver, or does this occur only with malnutrition?

And also, is cirrhosis of the liver a 'threshold phenomenon', i.e., is it caused only by consumption of more than a certain amount of alcohol per unit time, or does all the alcohol ingested cause some liver damage?

Current medical research indicates that cirrhosis of the liver (due to alcoholism) is caused not by malnutrition but ingestion of more alcohol than the liver can metabolize per unit time.

Alcohol is an example of a drug so widely used most people don't think of it as a drug. In moderation, the drug has beneficial tranquillizing effects. With larger doses, there is depression and slowing of reflexes. The 'stimulation' due to alcohol is actually caused by release of inhibitions.

The greatest drug problem faced by the United States today is due to alcohol. Forty per cent of all first time admissions to state hospitals are due to alcoholism. And about half of all murders and fatal traffic accidents occur under the influence of alcohol.

Addiction to the drug is common. When an alcoholic's supply is cut off, delirium tremens (D Ts) may occur, with death a not uncommon result.

Most authorities would consider you an alcoholic. Cut down on your consumption while you can.

Heroin

While camping near Big Sur recently, I met a young couple from Los Angeles. They had read my column in the L.A. *Free Press* and during the course of our conversation, the girl told me they had used 'smack' or heroin several times in the past few weeks. When I asked whether they weren't afraid of becoming addicted she replied, 'Oh no, smack isn't as addicting as people say. We can take it or leave it.'

Narcotics are drugs which relieve pain and produce sleep or

stupor. Heroin is one of the most potent narcotics and is used for medical reasons legally in some countries, notably Great Britain.* But its use is prohibited in the USA because the potential for addiction is greater than for narcotics like morphine. Since the drug is illegal, all heroin in the USA is, almost by definition, impure and often contaminated with fungi and bacteria.

Addiction to heroin does not result from its occasional use. Three or four weeks of daily or almost daily use is usually required before the user is hooked. The first time heroin is injected into a vein, the user will most likely be nauseated, feel faint and, in general, wonder why he's not getting any 'high' from the drug. With further use, he'll experience pleasurable sensations which have been described as an orgasm spreading all through the body. But frequent use of heroin results in tolerance, or the need to take increasingly larger amounts of the drug in order to produce the same effects.

Typically, the heroin user does not become addicted until after several months of sporadic use. But as the frequency of its use increases, there comes a time when he can no longer distinguish between the pleasure he desires from the drug and the physiological need which marks addiction. Once tolerance is developed, the heroin user will suffer from a classic set of withdrawal symptoms if he attempts to discontinue the drug.

*In Great Britain, while its use is not banned, it may not be prescribed for or given to addicts other than at a recognized addiction centre. The effects of this are three-fold:
1) Addicts who are registered at an addiction centre are not treated as criminals (see Dr Schoenfeld's last paragraph).
2) What illegal use there is derives its supply largely from oversubscription to registered addicts: hence economically motivated black-marketeers are not encouraging heroin use for their own profit.
3) Impure heroin is therefore not a common feature of the scene.

WITHDRAWAL SYMPTOMS

If a narcotic addict stops taking his drug, no signs will be apparent for about half a day. Then he'll become restless, nervous, and, at the same time, sleepy. Later, he'll perspire, his eyes will tear, and he'll have a runny nose. As time passes he becomes more and more restless, tossing and turning and twitching his arms and legs. He feels alternately warm and chilled. The pupils of his eyes are dilated, waves of gooseflesh travel over his body and he has painful muscle cramps. Vomiting and diarrhoea are common. The acute withdrawal symptoms last three to five days but for weeks or months afterwards he may suffer from anxiety and insomnia.

SHORTENED LIFE

The life expectancy of a heroin addict is much shorter than for the average person of his age group. One estimate is five years from the time he becomes hooked.

A heroin user can die or become seriously ill in several ways. The fastest is from an overdose of the drug; the same quantity needed to maintain an addict may be fatal when injected by a novice. Bad or grossly impure heroin is another quick way to die.

The most common serious disease of those using needles illegally is serum hepatitis. Boiling the needles will not necessarily kill the causative virus, but hepatitis, a disease of the liver, can surely kill a needle head. Other common maladies are abscesses and thrombophlebitis. The stigmata of the addict are 'tracks' or line-like scars over his veins.

MEDICAL TREATMENT?

Most heroin addicts seeking medical treatment wish to cut down the use of the drug simply because they can't afford the habit any longer (the cost of heroin may run as high as seventy-five dollars a day as tolerance increases). After their savings are gone, they may start selling their possessions. Many addicts turn to petty or major theft, or to prostitution. But violent acts of crime committed by addicts are rare because generally they are passive individuals, hung-up as much on the needle as on the drug. Many psychiatrists believe the act of pushing a needle into a vein has direct sexual significance.

More and more physicians are beginning to wonder why the user of heroin is treated as a criminal, subject to long terms in prison or prison hospitals. Physicians are forbidden by law to treat narcotic addicts as outpatients. If they are treated as in-patients, the hospital must report the case to the police.

Cough Syrups

Dear Dr Schoenfeld:
You have have answered this at one time or another, but what about Romilar and the other cough syrups with dextromethorphan in them? I've had about fifteen bottles in the last year – generally with good results and no real bummers. It doesn't seem to be doing me any harm.

Sincerely yours,
Harvey S—

Dr Schoenfeld:
I recently, on the advice of my friends, drank a bottle of Romilar C.F. cough syrup. This was supposed to get me stoned. It did just that. After about twenty minutes my arms and legs got limp. I could hardly think and slurred when I talked. I laid down and found myself hallucinating.

About an hour later, I got real sick and threw up, after which I couldn't walk. My pupils almost covered my whole iris. I went to bed that night and found myself hallucinating in double vision with my eyes open. The next day I had chattering teeth and every time I took a deep breath, I would end up yawning which would make my whole body go limp. I feel fine now (three days later).

Is what I did illegal?

Dear Mr B——:
I first heard about dextromethorphan cough syrups and tablets used for 'highs' from a British ex-commando in Copenhagen in 1965. Apparently, it hadn't appreciably benefited the ex-commando. He often went about bopping peaceful Danes on the chin in pubs such as Laurits Betjent and the Pilegaarden.

Recently, I treated a girl who had taken half a bottle of such a cough syrup at a rock dance As a result, she was semi-comatose, incontinent of urine, and required hospitalization. Her boyfriend, who had taken the same amount, seemed normal, except for dilated pupils.

Nothing is known about possible long-term harmful effects after frequently using large amounts of dextromethorphan. You're missing the point if your chief concern about this incident is whether or not you violated a statute.

Sincerely,
Eugene Schoenfeld, M.D.

Incensed

(The following letter was sent air mail special delivery from New Orleans.)
Dear Dr Schoenfeld:
Is it true that smoking incense can make you high? (I am mainly referring to the Joss incense sticks from India.)

Love,
Paul—

Dear Paul:

I have not been aware that smoking incense could make one high. This effect would have been discovered thousands of years ago if it were true.

Are you sure it's incense you're smoking?

Sincerely,
Eugene Schoenfeld, M.D.

Mescaline

Doctor Schoenfeld:
What are the effects of mescalin? Are there any bad ones? Is there any safe hallucinogen?
I'd appreciate an answer!

Thanks,
Larry M—

The effects of mescalin are well described in Aldous Huxley's *The Doors of Perception* and in *The Varieties of Psychedelic Experience* by Masters and Houston. In brief, mescaline is a mind-altering or psychedelic drug originally derived from peyote but now synthesized. When ingested in quantities approximating 2mgm/lb, mescalin produces a twelve-to-fourteen-hour alteration of sight, smell, touch, and hearing, with little of the internal reorganization caused by LSD. Though experience with the drug is limited, compared with LSD, bad trips seem to be extremely rare. No harmful physiological effects are known.

Recent animal experiments indicate that mescalin, like any drug, may be harmful to the unborn foetus, especially early in pregnancy.

No drugs, including hallucinogens, are completely 'safe'. Aspirin is probably the most commonly used and widely available drug, yet more children are killed by aspirin each year than by any other chemical.

Button, Button

Dear Dr Schoenfeld:
I would like to know what effects peyote could have on a person.
Does peyote cause any known damage to the body?

Sincerely,
Cactus Sam

From the way you signed your name I assume you know that peyote 'buttons' grow on the mescal cactus which is found in the southwestern United States. Since antiquity, American Indians have used peyote in their religious ceremonies.

The active ingredient of peyote is mescalin, a psychedelic drug used in the late nineteenth century by respected scientists such as William James and Havelock Ellis. More recently, authors Aldous Huxley and Robert Graves have extolled the virtues of mescalin.

Psychedelic connoisseurs claim subtle differences exist between peyote and mescalin. Both drugs cause changes in sensory perception, especially visual and tactile. The effects last approximately ten hours but there is little of the internal reorganization caused by drugs such as L S D. The effects wear off gradually and no period of recovery is usually required. With unsupervised use, untoward reactions are possible but seem to be extremely rare.

The use of peyote as a religious sacrament is sanctioned by law for members of the Native American Church. A fascinating account of a peyote ceremony was written recently by Stewart Brand for the *Psychedelic Review*.

Mushrooms and Toadstools

Last weekend my boyfriend and I were picking mushrooms in the woods and found some funny yellow ones with long stems. Could these have been the hallucinogenic mushrooms I've read about?

Before you go tripping off to the woods again, you should realize that only experts can distinguish between edible mushrooms and poisonous toadstools. Toadstools cause hallucinations, it's true, but death often follows.

So-called 'magic mushrooms' are grown in Mexico and used for religious purposes by descendants of the Aztecs. Psilocybe mexicana (the scientific name for the mushroom) causes coloured visions, body-image changes, and hallucinations when ingested in suitable quantities. The active ingredient is psilocybin.

Quick Trip

Could you please advise me on the effects and possible dangers encountered in the use of the drug D M T?

D M T, or dimethylTRYPtamine, has been called the 'business man's psychedelic' because its effects last only from five to thirty minutes. The experience approximates an L S D trip except that it is an almost instantaneous high because it is usually mixed with tobacco or marijuana and inhaled (it is not effective when ingested).

Like most hallucinogens, potential harmful effects are largely unknown, perhaps due to the lack of extensive clinical investigations. Some individuals might possibly have a bad psychological reaction because of the rapid onset of effects as opposed to the forty-five to ninety minute delay after ingestion of LSD.

On the other hand, the effects of DMT wear off quickly with little of the slow process of mental reorganization found after LSD use.

Since DMT is not commercially available, the drug offered for sale is illegally produced and thus may contain impurities, the harm of which is impossible to assess because of differences in the technical skill and equipment of the illicit manufacturer.

Peruvian Indians of the Waiku tribe extract a hallucinogenic compound from the sap of trees in their vicinity. This hallucinogen has a chemical structure similar to DMT. When dried, powdered, and used as snuff it produces a thirty-to-sixty-minute trip.

The Waiku use a long wooden tube to blow the snuff high into the nasal passages of their brethren, allowing coverage of a much larger area of the nasal passage lining which absorbs the snuff. Thus they literally and figuratively blow their minds.

MDA

There's been a lot of talk lately about a new drug called MDA. What are its effects? Do the initials MDA mean anything or are they another put-on like the STP initials?

MDA is methylenedioxyamphetamine, a mind-altering drug derived from amphetamine. Both drugs were first synthesized (amphetamine in 1933) by Gordon Alles, who died recently in California.

MDA is an example of a mind-altering drug apparently specific to certain functions of the brain. If the LSD experience can be described as one including both perceptual or sensory changes and inner experiences such as insight, the effects of MDA could be said to be similar to LSD with few of the sensory changes. In other words, illusions and other changes in perceiving 'reality' are infrequent or absent with the use of M D A. The drug is said to promote harmonious interpersonal relationships.

M D A has not been extensively tested in humans and may have unrecognized harmful effects, as with any unproven drug. Moreover the M D A available on the black market may contain impurities.

Hawaiian Trip

Dr Schoenfeld:
I have in the past engaged in a woodrose trip following the old Hawaiian tradition of using the seeds of a woodrose tree as a native turn-on. What is it in woodrose that makes one high? Does it contain anything toxic?

Woodrose seeds contain L S D-like compounds that produce a similar psychedelic experience. The same precautions which apply to L S D are true for woodrose trips. In addition, nausea and vomiting almost always are part of the experience.

Nutmeg

Dear Dr Schoenfeld:
Since my occasional use of nutmeg, I have been having vivid hallucinations from local anaesthetics (Novocaine, Xylocaine), which, properly speaking, are not hallucinogens at all. This has never occurred during previous operations, prior to my experimenting with nutmeg. A friend who uses L S D has had this type of occurrence also. What are the perils attendant on usage of nutmeg?
Yours sincerely,
Stephen B—

Several reports have appeared in medical journals about nutmeg intoxication in college students. One or two hours after ingestion there is a leaden feeling in the arms and legs, agitation, apprehension, and feelings of depersonalization and unreality. Symptoms mimicking belladonna poisoning may occur, such as dry mouth, thirst, a rapid heartbeat, and a red flushed face. Nausea and vomiting may accompany the above.

Myristicin is one of the principal oils in nutmeg and probably is responsible for most of the effects of nutmeg intoxication, but the full spectrum of symptoms may depend on other substances present. In animal experiments, large doses of myristicin produce severe liver damage.

Hallucinations associated with local anaesthetics are unusual and, to my knowledge, not related to nutmeg or L S D. If any readers have had similar experiences I would like to know of them.

Poppers

Dear Doctor:
I have recently discovered the effects of a drug called amyl nitrite, generally sold in glass vials known as 'poppers'. The vial is broken and the escaping vapour is inhaled deeply to produce a rapid, intense, but short-lived high (five minutes or so).

Several of my friends and I use poppers (a couple of times a week, seldom more than two in an evening). We frequently use them during sex. We should like to know whether the drug is dangerous in any way.

Linda C—

Amyl nitrite is a drug used in the treatment of angina pectoris, or pain resulting from constriction of the coronary arteries of the heart. The drug is available in mesh-covered capsules or 'poppers'.

When the capsule is 'popped' or crushed and the contents inhaled, coronary and other blood vessels are dilated or enlarged, thus allowing a greater flow of blood. The dilatation is responsible for a flush (both felt and observable) which gives the sensation of a brief, sensual high.

If amyl nitrite is used excessively, there is the possibility of causing methhaemoglobinaemia, a potentially dangerous condition in which blood cells change colour and give the skin a cyanotic or blue appearance.

The most commonly noted ill effects are headache, dizziness, weakness, and a severe bronchitis.

Heavenly Blue

Dr Schoenfeld:
Recently I have been getting a mild high on morning-glory seeds (compared to a 250 microgram LSD tab). Is this known to be dangerous? Are there precautions other than the usual?

Love,
A girl who has to know

Morning-glory seeds contain ololiuqui which is basically lysergic acid monoethylamide, a compound very similar to LSD. Packagers of morning-glory seeds now coat the seeds with a substance which causes severe nausea and vomiting.

When the hallucinogenic properties of the previously pristine morning-glory became known, legislation was considered which would have outlawed this new found 'menace'. But the spectre arose of FDA agents swooping down on blue-haired LOLs puttering in their gardens.

Fortunately, the public was spared the expense of putting yet another unenforceable law on the books. And law officials were also spared because when one law is freely and knowingly violated, disrespect is created for all other laws.

STP

What can you tell me about STP? My roommate has been saving two tablets he says are STP for over a year and has offered to give me one of them.

The initials 'STP' have no relation to the drug's chemical formula, which is methyl dimethoxy methyl phenylethylamine. STP was reportedly chosen as a popular name because of its put-on potential.

STP was first synthesized by chemist Alexander Shulgin, Ph.D., who was working for Dow Chemical at the time. The drug is said to produce a psychedelic experience more intense than LSD and lasting three times as long.

When the drug first appeared on the black market in the spring of 1967, about one per cent of its users required treatment in clinics and hospitals. This apparently resulted from placing twice the 'recommended' dose in each tablet (20mgm vs 10mgm).

Treatment of bad STP trips should be conducted with caution. At least one death was reported from the combination of STP and chlorpromazine (Thorazine). Perhaps the drug which indirectly caused the death was not STP (belladonna, for example, is often pushed as a psychedelic drug); in any case, no phenothiazine should be used for treating STP trips. These include Thorazine, Compazine, Stelazine, Prolixin, Largon, Permitil, Sparine, and Tindal.*

*STP is incompatible with certain drugs in common everyday use in this country as sedatives and tranquillizers, Largactil, Sparine for example. Death may occur if the two are taken at the same time or within a short period of each other.

Legal High

Can you recommend a legal way to expand one's consciousness?

Find a mate you can groove with. You'll then have an additional brain and set of sensory organs. The quantity of your experience will be at least doubled and the quality will differ because no two people perceive in exactly the same manner. With a warm, sensitive, perceptive mate you'll be able to freely give and receive love.

Tale of Hoffman

Can you tell me when and how LSD was discovered?

Like many important scientific discoveries, L S D was the result of equal quantities of painstaking, tedious research, and luck. Two Swiss Sandoz scientists, Stoll and Hoffman, first synthesized L S D in 1938 while studying ergot derivatives, drugs which have the effect of contracting the uterus and which are also used in the treatment of migraine headaches.

They found in animal experiments that L S D was similar in its uterine stimulatory effects to other ergot preparations and not very interesting in this respect. Later, Hoffman became interested in L S D because of its molecular resemblance to nikethamide, a central nervous system stimulant. While doing research with L S D in his laboratory, Hoffman had an unusual experience which he described as follows:

In the afternoon of 16 April 1943, when I was working on this problem, I was seized by a peculiar sensation of vertigo and restlessness. Objects, as well as the shape of my associates in the laboratory, appeared to undergo optical changes. I was unable to concentrate on my work. In a dream-like state I left for home where an irresistible urge to lie down overcame me. I drew the curtains and immediately fell into a peculiar state similar to a drunkenness, characterized by an exaggerated imagination.

With my eyes closed, fantastic pictures of extraordinary plasticity and intensive color seemed to surge toward me. After two hours this state gradually wore off.

Hoffman realized he had accidentally ingested or inhaled a small quantity of L S D. Now he decided to intentionally ingest the drug. Using known safe doses of other ergot derivatives as a guide, he took what he thought would be a small quantity, 250 micrograms. His reaction to this dose was even more spectacular.

L S D has been praised as a panacea for all man's ills and damned as a threat to the survival of society as we know it. One thing seems certain. L S D or similar drugs will provide the most important clues to understanding man and his relation to his environment since the teachings of Sigmund Freud.

Freud knew there was a physiologic basis for the functions of the brain but could not elucidate the process. The discovery that chemicals can profoundly alter and mimic the 'normal' and 'pathologic' processes of the brain will eventually lead psychiatry toward treatment methods more effective than any presently known.

Name Brand

About four months ago, I had a quantity of Purple Owsley LSD tabs with which I immediately turned on all my friends. I've been saving two of them for a very special occasion but they are turning a pale colour and it looks like all the purple is disappearing. What causes this? Will it still be as potent as when the colour was darker?

The change in colour may indicate decomposition of the L S D as well as the food-colouring agent; the resulting product may cause effects even less predictable than the 'pure' original.

How can you be certain they are Owsley tablets? He has told me his name is often used as a means of selling drugs (because Owsley has become synonymous with quality drugs).

L S D Liver

Dear Dr Schoenfeld:
Is it safe for a person with a liver problem to take L S D? I have heard it puts a strain on the liver and may cause trouble. Still, I've talked with other people who say friends have just recovered from hepatitis and dropped acid without complications. How does acid get involved with the liver anyway?

Truly yours,
Velma—

Dear Velma:
The metabolism of L S D after ingestion is still largely a mystery but it may be partially broken down by the liver. That is the reason for the concern about L S D straining an already damaged liver.

No one knows at this time if a damaged liver will be further harmed by L S D though the minute quantity involved makes this seem unlikely.

Sincerely,
Eugene Schoenfeld, M.D.

Bloody Lie

In school we were told that when L S D was put in a jar of human blood, after a certain amount of time the chromosomes in the blood were destroyed. They also said that this destruction was evident in blood samples taken from acid-heads and that their offspring will be mutants. Is this true?

To say that you were told half-truths would be an exaggeration.

Studies made of the effect of L S D on chromosomes have given conflicting results. Half the studies conclude that L S D causes changes in cell chromosomes while the others have shown no change in cell chromosomes of L S D users. One of the latter studies was published in the 27 October 1967 *Science*, but received little attention by the news media.

The meaning of cell chromosome changes, if they occur, is even more obscure. No authority in the field has ever said that the alleged chromosomal changes had caused harm to L S D users. Some believe that the chromosomes appear similar to those found in certain types of leukaemia, but no case of leukaemia has ever been linked to L S D use.

One case has been reported of a mother taking L S D three times during pregnancy and bearing a deformed child. If the use of L S D prior to pregnancy led to birth defects we could expect an epidemic similar to the thalidomide disaster, but this is not the case. No drug (including L S D) should be taken *during* pregnancy except on the advice of a physician, lest harm be done to the unborn child.*

Acid and Joints

After a recent session with acid, I noticed severe pain in the joints of my knees, my neck, and my groin.
Is this common, is it me, or is it the acid?

*L S D is not in common use in this country either legally (only in certain mental hospitals) or illegally, and in both areas its use seems to be on the decline at the moment. Hence British doctors' knowledge of the drug and its real or alleged effects, either psychological – after a bad trip – or physical is almost certainly extremely vague.

LSD users have often reported muscle cramps and aching in the joints under the effects of the drug. Whether this is due to the effects of LSD or whether the user moves about less than he does usually is unclear.

I have observed similar effects in Africans given the hallucinogenic root *Tabernanthe Iboga*. At intervals during ceremonial dances, the limbs of the patient are stretched, apparently to prevent muscle cramps.

Fathers and LSD

Dr Schoenfeld:
In an article on the dangers of LSD causing birth defects in babies whose mothers had taken the drug, it failed to mention anything about the father of the child.

If the mother has never taken it but the father has, and assuming that the chromosomes have been changed or damaged, can abnormalities in the child still result from the father's use?

Thank you

In theory, abnormalities in the child could result from damaged chromosomes in the father. But this has never happened despite the hundreds of thousands or millions of prospective fathers who have taken LSD trips.

Gross changes in chromosomes would more likely result in sterility than malformations. Despite the scare stories, neither an increase in congenital defects nor a decreased birth rate has been shown among LSD users.*

*With respect to Dr Schoenfeld, I find it difficult to believe that even in America there are 'millions' of fathers or prospective fathers who have taken LSD, and to this extent I am unhappy that it should be so readily accepted that no congenital defects or other problems can be expected to be associated with it.

L. A. Acid

Dr Schoenfeld:
I live in the Los Angeles area and I know several people who have taken LSD. I also know people who have taken what is called acid. Around here they seem to be two different things. The acid makes you lose all sense of depth and you see things wavy and in fours. In all of the magazine articles I have read, this kind of acid has never been mentioned. Could you please tell me the difference and all of the effects and facts.

Thank you,
Mixed Up

'Acid' is slang for LSD, but perhaps your friends are taking different drugs. Since all the LSD found in the 'street' is illegally manufactured, different batches may contain impurities giving varied effects.

Some drug experts believe bad trips would be reduced if pure LSD were used rather than street LSD.

Acid Drops Baby

Purely by accident, my third child was born two weeks premature while I was under the influence of LSD. What effect, if any, might this have on the child, now or in the future? The child is presently 5 months old and seems to be in normal health. Has this occurred before, and if so, what effect has this had on other children? I personally feel the birth was much easier for me.

Perhaps it was not purely by accident that your child was born prematurely while you were under the influence of LSD. LSD is derived from ergot, a drug sometimes used to induce labour late in pregnancy.

LSD has been taken during delivery by other women according to several reports, none published as far as I know. This is certainly not recommended because while the mother might have a good trip, the effects on the baby are unknown. But in all likelihood your child will be perfectly normal. There is no evidence yet to believe otherwise.

Birth Defects and LSD

I took 350 micrograms of LSD and a week later learned that I was pregnant. Will I have a deformed child? Please answer quickly.

Any drug, including aspirin and caffeine, may increase the risk of bearing a child with congenital defects. When injected into rats at a critical point early in pregnancy, both caffeine and LSD apparently can cause an increase in stillbirths, miscarriages, and deformities.

In humans, LSD has not been shown to cause an increase in birth defects, despite the horror stories you may have read. Its effect on future generations is unknown; the same holds true for the hundreds of other drugs introduced in recent years.

The chances are that you will have a healthy, normal baby. But, as I have said many times, no drug should be taken during pregnancy except on the advice of a physician.

Dangers of LSD

Some of my friends have taken literally dozens of beautiful acid trips with no apparent bad results. Can you comment on the possible dangers of LSD?

LSD available 'on the street' is illegally manufactured and you have no way of knowing whether the drug you purchase contains pure L S D, imperfect L S D, or has added to it belladonna, methamphetamine, or other drugs.

Some black-market chemists, who sincerely believed their manufacture of L S D was a public service, switched from capsules to tablets when they found small dealers were cutting or diluting the capsules. But even tablets may be pulverized and repressed.

Let's assume for the moment that you could obtain pure Sandoz L S D. There is no absolute way of knowing who will have a good trip and who will flip out.

Some voyagers have taken L S D hundreds of times with no apparent harm. Others have taken the drug dozens of times, all beautiful trips, but on the next journey they flip out and are hospitalized. Individuals have been hospitalized after only one L S D experience.

No one knows the incidence of bad trips because the drug is illegal. The most recent scientific evidence indicates that most people having prolonged adverse reactions to L S D have a previous history of psychiatric illness.

Several reports linking L S D use with cell chromosome abnormalities have received widespread newspaper and magazine publicity. An equal number of reports showing no chromosome damage among L S D users have received practically no publicity (*Science*, 27 October 1967, and 16 February 1968).

L S D Therapy

I have dropped acid several times and have gained a certain degree of insight into some of my psychic problems.

However, I would like to confine further exploration to a therapeutic situation. Can you give me the name of a psychiatrist who uses L S D as an adjunct of therapy?

All the legal L S D in the United States is controlled strictly by the Food and Drug Administration (F D A) and the National

Institute of Mental Health (N I M H). Consequently, the drug may be used for research and treatment only after careful evaluation by N I M H. Rumour has it that permission for research is denied to those scientists who admit personal use of L S D.

Float Downstream

Dr Schoenfeld:
Soon after my first L S D trip, I was pleased to notice that a chronic pain which had persisted in my right lung since a bout with pneumonia seven years ago, had disappeared. Also, a minor but chronic face rash has lately been fading away!

My friends think I am putting them on. What do you think, Doc, am I deluded or what?

Best regards,
Ed—

Dear Ed:
Deluded or not, your face rash has been fading and the pain in your lung has disappeared.

Whatever the causes, you seem to be, at the moment, better off now than you were before.

Stay where you are.

Sincerely,
Eugene Schoenfeld, M.D.

Family Dog

(The following letter was written on the back of a computer print-out sheet.)
Do you treat humans only or also animals (pup-dogs) as well? The reason we (I) ask is that we have recently acquired a 2-month-old pup-tad. One question is: We are having trouble house-

breaking this pup dog. . . Her name being Ruby Tuesday because she's ornry.

Also, we wail quite a lot, and we want to know if Ruby is too young to join us, that is, will she suffer brain damage or stunt her growth.

Incidentally, she's an Aquarian (if you need this data for your diagnosis). Please don't tell the narks on us.

Love,
Name Withheld

P.S. *When will she be old enough for her first acid trip and how much should we give her?*

Animal experiments have shown that dogs and cats do indeed have hallucinations when given L S D and other hallucinogens. But the nature of their experiences is largely unknown to us except by observation of their behaviour. An animal given L S D might be terrified since he could not know that his trip was precipitated by a drug. L S D, in normal hallucinogenic doses (the quantity depends on the animal species and weight) has not, thus far, been known to cause brain damage or retard growth.

Your questions were referred to a local veterinarian who informed me that a 2-month-old puppy is equivalent in age to a 2-year-old child. I don't think L S D should be given to children and he feels the same way about puppies.

Uncool

My parents will be visiting me in the near future. Do you think it would be wise for me to turn them on using marijuana and/or L S D in cakes, soups, Kool-Aid, etc. and not tell them? My father, age 58, is a diabetic. My mother has high blood-pressure.

A loving son

If you are serious about putting LSD and/or marijuana in food without informing those who are ingesting the food, you are about to commit a criminal as well as a most foolish and dangerous act. I hope you were joking in your letter.

People who are turned on to mind-altering drugs without their knowledge may think they are losing their minds and this may precipitate a true psychosis.

Sincerely,
Eugene Schoenfeld, M.D.

The Killer Weed

Mrs Garnet Brennan, 58-year-old principal of a grade school in Nicasio, California, was recently fired by her school board after a thirty-year record of devoted and excellent teaching to her students. This action was taken because of her sworn affidavit that she had smoked marijuana almost daily for the past eighteen years, apparently with no harmful effects (the affidavit was one of hundreds collected for the defence of another Marin County resident, charged with the sale of marijuana).

Not only did the lady state the drug had not harmed her but she added that marijuana had helped her become a more effective teacher (she denied ever having turned on during school hours).

This story was front-page news for several days and shocked those who had associated marijuana use only with musicians, hippies and, occasionally, ballet dancers. Mrs Brennan may be a hippie at heart but she is also a homeowner in Forest Knolls, a semi-rural Marin County suburb where many residents still use the horse as a means of transportation. She has always been considered a model citizen and teacher by her friends, neighbours, and co-workers.

Mrs Brennan was fired because she admitted to having broken the law enacted to protect you and me from the alleged harmful effects of marijuana. Ideally, laws are based on reason and the most complete information available bearing on the issue at hand. With this in mind, I would like to present some medical facts pertaining to marijuana.

According to the most widely used pharmacology reference work, Goodman and Gilman's *Pharmacological Basis of Therapeutics*, Third Edition: 'There are no lasting ill effects from the acute use of marijuana and no fatalities have ever been recorded.'

Not that bad reactions to marijuana are completely unknown. Emotionally unstable individuals may freak out after using the drug even in small quantities. Diabetics may be more vulnerable to insulin reactions. Rarely are there allergic reactions to marijuana. But in normal people there are no known harmful medical effects resulting from its use (and the first recorded medical reference to marijuana was in the herbal of the Chinese Emperor Shen Nung more than 4,600 years ago).

What about its behavioural effects? Many law enforcement officials claim marijuana use leads to violent acts of crime. But according to Goodman and Gilman, 'violent or aggressive behaviour, however, is infrequent'. Could the same be said of alcohol?

It has also been claimed that long-term use of marijuana causes permanent (and presumably undesirable) changes in the personality. A physician from Greece (that land of free thought) was invited to the USA recently to give his views of chronic marijuana use. Typical of his statements was one in which he claimed he could spot a chronic user two blocks away by his walk. Imagine then Mrs Brennan using her new-found and unwelcome leisure time to vacation in Athens. While strolling through Constitution Square she is seized by the Greek police who have spotted the characteristic marijuana walk. Back to reality.

'The influence of marijuana on intellectual functions and on emotional reactions and general personality structure was studied by Halpern (1944) who concluded that basic personality structure is not changed and that thoughts or emotions totally alien to the individual are not aroused by the drug.' (Goodman and Gilman again.)

The lack of evidence showing marijuana to be harmful or addicting may have a tendency to cause impairment of judgement in some who have a large stake in maintaining the present laws. I recently appeared on a radio programme with an attorney and a narcotics agent to discuss the marijuana issue. This agent, who directs operations over a large area of California, said, 'If I had a 17-year-old daughter, I'd rather see her on heroin than marijuana.'

Grasping at straws aptly describes the most recent argument advanced by marijuanaphobes. They admit that marijuana is not physically harmful or addicting but say that its use leads to 'psychological dependence'. One develops 'psychological dependence' towards many things – art, music, automobiles, vacations, friends, etc. To quote Goodman and Gilman for the last time, 'An overwhelming preoccupation with the continued use of marijuana is an extreme rarity.'

Medical Letter is a periodical noted for its objective judgement of drugs. Its 22 September 1967 issue dealt, in part, with marijuana: 'There is no evidence that it has any physiological or emotional effects which directly lead to more serious drug abuse, but its use may facilitate contact with persons or groups using more dangerous drugs.' Which is another way of saying that millions of Americans who use marijuana must obtain the drug from dealers who very well may be handling and promoting truly dangerous drugs. The present marijuana laws have not only created a whole new 'criminal' class of otherwise productive citizens, but they encourage disrespect for all laws.

Mrs Brennan confessed to a drug habit more serious than her use of marijuana in her now-famous affidavit. She said she could hardly wait until breaks between classes so that she could smoke a cigarette or two. Cigarettes are addictive, cause lung cancer and emphysema, and contribute to the development of heart disease and peptic ulcers. I hope Mrs Brennan can some-day kick this vicious habit.

No Place Like Home

I have already discovered two small worms and a tiny red ant-like insect in my grass. Before I roll a joint I try to check through the quantity I am using but the creatures are so small that it would be unrealistic to depend upon complete success in finding and elimi-nating them. Is there any reason why I should not continue to use the grass? It would be such a shame to throw it away.

Occasionally I will read a letter (omitting name) before a hos-pital conference. A psychiatric nurse asked whether you see these insects before or after smoking your grass.

One wonders about insects that nest in and feed upon mari-juana. What is their reality?

Albert Schweitzer would have reminded you of the necessity of Reverence for Life. He instructed his staff never to needless-ly harm animals, including insects. His workers would lift wheelbarrows rather than run them over lines of ants. He used antibiotics to save human lives but pointed out harmless as well as harmful bacteria were being destroyed.

Perhaps you could find a way to spare the lives of the insects in your grass. You represent more harm to them than they to you.

A University of California graduate student speculates, 'I imagine them at home in their grass world munching on parti-cularly resinous bits of leaves or gnawing on a stem. Suddenly they are sent tumbling and packed firmly into a cylinder. They sense strange forces acting upon them, a strong wind followed by heat and fire. They and their world are consumed and trans-formed as they enter and transform your world.'

(Insects living in houses made of Gold are apparently not a rarity. And not everyone is put up-tight by them, judging from the following letter.)

Dear Dr Schoenfeld:
My husband and I accidentally discovered one of God's most enchanting creatures while preparing some grass on a sheet of white paper. It was a sort of inch-worm, an absurdly minute dot upon the cosmic scale. And from the way it danced and frolicked and whirled and spun and bowed and pranced, it was obvious that its environment had made it a sort of superbug.

That little speck of life was grooving on everything; the white paper, the light, the grass, the vibrations in the air. We watched him for a full half hour, taking in the whole sermon.

And put him back, carefully, of course . . . and we reverently hope that little creature is still in there somewhere – stoned and joyful – and that someday we'll lift him out for another performance.

I would say his reality has a lot more going for him than ours.
Love

Marijuana and Epilepsy

Is the smoking of marijuana dangerous to an epileptic? Quite a few years ago, I suffered two mild epileptic seizures and I am very interested to find out if smoking grass could bring about another attack.

Marijuana is a known long-acting anticonvulsant. Should more research be permitted the drug might prove to be valuable in treating certain types of epilepsy. But at present the answer is not definitely known.

(Author's note: I have received several telephone calls from epileptics who claimed they had used marijuana frequently without apparent harm. One caller said the drug had decreased his seizures. The following letter was received shortly after the above question appeared in print.)

Dear Dr Schoenfeld:
I was interested in the question submitted by a reader concerning the possible effects of marijuana on epileptics. I too am an epileptic (grand mal). However, I have not had any seizures since my first attack two years ago. I continue to take medication (Dilantin) for my illness.

I have smoked marijuana several times in the past two years and have never experienced any ill effects.

I just thought I would pass this information on to you since others may be curious about the effect of marijuana upon their neurological system.

Driving on the Grass

I can't drive at all while high because the road hypnotizes me, but my husband claims to feel in control while stoned behind the wheel. God knows driving is maddeningly dangerous enough when straight.

We love our kids and want to stay with them. So are we compounding our chances of an accident to drive while high? I don't see how anyone could have scientific proof but could you give us an educated guess anyway?

There certainly are scientific methods for measuring drug-induced changes in reflexes and perception of depth and distance. Alcohol, for example, has been shown to drastically impair one's faculties. But similar tests have not yet been performed on those under the influence of marijuana.

As your letter points out, many people feel they can drive well under the influence of marijuana. But some people feel the same way about alcohol.

We may have some empirical evidence when the reported 500,000 pothead GIs return from Vietnam.

Lower Tar Content?

Can you tell me please if smoking marijuana can cause the same type of lung damage that smoking tobacco does?

Is there a tar in marijuana which coats the lungs, as in tobacco? Or is there something which might be even worse?

No one really knows whether the chronic use of marijuana might be as harmful to the lungs as the chronic use of tobacco.

Most cigarette heads smoke from twenty to forty tobacco joints daily. Since the effects of inhaled marijuana last from one-and-a-half to three hours, the consumption of an equivalent quantity would seem most unlikely.

Tars differ in their irritant and cancer-producing potentials so there remains the possibility that the chronic inhalation of marijuana smoke is more harmful than the chronic inhalation of larger quantities of tobacco. But there is no evidence to support this possibility.

Mouldy Bread

A month ago, I baked three loaves of hashish rye bread and put them in my refrigerator. One loaf is left but some mould grew on it. I cut off the mould but more might be in the loaf. Is there any danger involved if some of the mould is accidentally eaten?

Bread mould, though unsightly and perhaps unpalatable, is not harmful if ingested. Except for peanut mould (which may be carcinogenic), food moulds are apparently harmless.

Mouldy Grass

We have been moistening our grass and then putting it away in a warm place until a white and eventually blue-green mould appears. This seems to alter the effect considerably (for the better). What kind of mould is it and can it do any harm?

It is probably a happy mould. Positive identification of moulds is usually possible only by direct examination. A mycologist in the Botany Department of a college could make such an identification. Perhaps you've made an important discovery – after all penicillin was originally made from moulds. More likely the change you note is due to ageing of the marijuana. Some moulds are very harmful, especially when inhaled.

(Author's note: After the above answer appeared in print, I learned that many potheads were deliberately trying to grow mould on their marijuana, hoping to achieve the same effect.)

Pacifier?

My wife is nursing our new baby. Will any harm be caused the baby if she smokes marijuana now and then?

Like the answer to many other questions about marijuana, its distribution in the body after inhalation or ingestion is largely unknown. Its effect on babies is also unknown. But there is certainly a strong possibility it might be excreted in mother's milk. Your baby is on a good trip anyway when at its mother's breast and marijuana probably won't make it better. There is possible harm with the use of any drug. Why take a chance with your baby?

Israeli Bond

Is it possible to synthesize marijuana?

An Israeli scientist has synthesized a compound believed to have the same effects as marijuana. The chemical process is complicated and yields relatively small amounts of the 'plastic pot'.

The synthetic compound, tetrahydrocannabinol (THC), was not derived from any part of the cannabis sativa plant, thus it was exempt from the marijuana laws. Federal regulations, recently enacted, have made THC an illegal drug.

Contact

Is marijuana accumulated? In other words, can one become high without taking it again – sort of a self-induced recurrence?

Marijuana is not known to be accumulated in the body. Some people can turn on without drugs, but I believe you are referring to the phenomenon known as a 'contact' high. This has been often noted in groups of people when the euphoria or cheery vibrations of those stoned have an infectious effect on those who are straight. If you have these feelings when alone and they are unwanted you should consider psychiatric consultation.

Increased Awareness

I have colitis and when I smoke grass I feel some pain. Is the grass injuring the tissue or just sensitizing me to the pain?

Ulcerative colitis is an inflammatory disease of the lining of the colon. I suspect you are more sensitive to the discomfort of colitis when smoking marijuana. If you are not under the close supervision of a physician, you should be, since ulcerative colitis can be a most serious disease.

No Tolerance

Do the effects of marijuana become milder with continued use? I have been turning on for the past several months and I find myself hardly affected at all any more.

I would also like to know if one can become high from chewing marijuana seeds or just eating the stuff.

Tolerance to marijuana (the necessity to take more and more of the drug to achieve the same effect) does not occur from one day to the other. In other words, once the effects of the initial dose have fully worn off, the same amount of marijuana will produce the same results.

The effects of marijuana may vary greatly depending upon the type used. 'Acapulco Gold' was a recent hit song referring to a particularly strong 'brand' of marijuana grown in that region of Mexico. Other types said to be very powerful are Panama Red, Michoacan, Berkeley Boo, and Heyns Green (named after the Chancellor of the University of California at Berkeley, who one day discovered a number of marijuana plants mysteriously growing in his garden).

Some believe that weather and soil conditions greatly influence the kind of 'trip' given by the drug, i.e., contemplative, visual, etc. The fatigue-producing element of the drug also seems to vary, depending upon the type used. Even with the same type of marijuana, exposure to air, heat, light, moisture, etc. are all factors which may make the drug more or less potent.

Chewing marijuana seeds or eating the dried leaves can certainly produce a high, though the drug is more commonly eaten in cooked foods. The amount of marijuana one can smoke is limited by the tolerance of one's lungs to the smoke and one's ability (or desire) to reach for a joint once the effects of the drug have been made known. An Arab saying is that the cough indicates when enough of the drugs has been used.

When taken by mouth, the effects of marijuana are not felt for about one hour. Thus it is possible to take more of the drug than desired. Bad psychological reactions to marijuana are rare but they do occur and there are indications that they are more frequent as the amount of the drug used is increased.

Diabetes and Marijuana

I am 20 years old and have to take insulin daily for diabetes. I would like to try marijuana. Will this be harmful to me?

As you know, your insulin requirements depend a great deal on your caloric intake and the types of food you eat (i.e. high in sugar, fat, protein, etc.). Marijuana is a powerful stimulant to the appetite but the mechanism for this peculiar property is unclear since research studies have shown conflicting results.

One reports that marijuana raises blood sugar, another that it lowers blood sugar (perhaps the investigators were stoned).

Someday, marijuana or one of its components might be a proven valuable agent in the treatment of diabetes. It might be useful also in treating anorexia nervosa (a condition in which the victim may literally die from lack of appetite) or as an aid in psychotherapy. Meanwhile, it would be best for you to avoid marijuana since it might cause an insulin reaction by decreasing your blood sugar, or diabetic coma by raising it directly or via visits to candy counters in all-night food stores.

It is often apparent that drowsiness, increased hunger, and dryness of the mouth are incurred by smoking pot or hash. I have thought for a long time that this may be due to the fact that pot can cause a depression of the blood sugar. How or why this might be true I do not know. I do know, though, as a diabetic, that if I have smoked a large amount of pot or hash it is possible for me to have an insulin reaction. This may happen even when I have recently eaten a meal. Has this been noted before?

In the first HIP POCRATES column I pointed out that marijuana might be dangerous for diabetics, but yours is the first confirmation of this suspicion. I recently wrote to the *Journal of the American Medical Association* quoting your letter and adding, 'Though the use of marijuana is illegal in all states, millions of Americans have tried the drug and its use appears to be spreading rather than diminishing. In normal individuals its danger is more legal than medical. But marijuana does appear to be dangerous when used by diabetics because it alters their requirements for insulin, probably by lowering blood sugar. The component of marijuana which lowers blood sugar might be a useful hypoglycemic (blood-sugar lowering) agent and I suggest this would be a worthy area of research.'

Grass Allergy

My favourite tripping buddy has had headaches, earaches, post-nasal drips, and sore throats for the past eight to ten months. He has been tested for all sorts of pollens and food allergies with all tests negative. Allergy pills and/or abstinence from marijuana relieves the symptoms. Are there any reported instances of allergy to marijuana?

You bet your sweet kilo there are! Reports in the medical literature indicate that bronchitis, asthma, and allergic pneumonia can follow inhalation of marijuana smoke.

The surprising thing is that this particular allergy is relatively uncommon, otherwise antihistamine manufacturers and allergists would work themselves to death.

Pregnancy and Marijuana

During the first month of my pregnancy (and before I realized I was pregnant) I smoked marijuana twice and it has worried me ever since. Do you think this will have any effect on the pregnancy and/or the foetus?

I know of no reports linking the use of marijuana with disorders of pregnancy or birth defects. But no drug should be taken during pregnancy, especially the first three months, except on the specific advice of your physician. If marijuana did cause birth defects, one would expect an epidemic far surpassing the thalidomide disaster since there are millions of American females in the child-bearing age group who use or have used marijuana.

Marijuana Myth

I have heard that marijuana usage causes vitamin deficiencies. Can you tell me if this is so and if so what vitamins?

There are no known harmful effects from the use of marijuana in normal individuals. A vitamin deficiency coincident with the use of marijuana is probably the result of an inadequate diet such as some of the macrobiotic diets which are low in protein and devoid of such essentials as ascorbic acid or Vitamin C.

Smoke Screen

For not loving people my body sent me a stomach ulcer as a warning. I smoke grass regularly. It was one of my devices to shut out people or avoid facing things. Is it bad for an ulcer? Should I give up grass for the duration as I try to heal my soul and patch up my insides?

Current medical thought is that most peptic ulcers are caused by emotional tension or anxiety. An important part of the treatment of ulcers is the relief of tension through sedatives or tranquillizers. And one of the known effects of marijuana in most people is relief of tension. Its direct physical effects on the stomach are unknown.

If you frequently use marijuana to shut out people, even its staunchest advocates would say you are misusing the drug.

Escalation Theory

Some of my friends who use marijuana also use heroin. Does the use of marijuana lead to the use of narcotics?

Most heroin addicts use or have used marijuana. In this respect there is an association between the two, but they are not causally related. Heroin addicts usually graduate to narcotics from the use of alcohol. In terms of disease processes alone, alcoholism is a far worse malady than narcotics addiction.

The link between marijuana and heroin is that both are illegal drugs, use of either of which is subject to severe penalties.

Although penalties for the use of marijuana and heroin are similar, it should not be assumed that the non-addictive properties of marijuana apply to heroin and other narcotics.

Heroin is one of the most addictive narcotics and regular use will surely lead to physiological addiction within four weeks. Anyone who risks addiction to drugs, legal or otherwise, which will cause him to spend much of his time finding means to pay for his habit is most uncool.

The Felons

I was recently convicted of possession of marijuana and received three years probation. As part of my probation I must submit to regular urinalysis and Nalline tests. I am told that amphetamines and hard narcotics are readily detected by these tests but that marijuana isn't.

I don't care for anything besides marijuana now and then. Can you tell me whether these tests can detect marijuana usage and if so, how long after one gets high?

Love,
A Very Worried Pothead

Dr Schoenfeld:
My probation department recently dropped its Nalline testing programme in favour of a urinalysis programme.

I have been told that most drugs can be detected by careful urinalysis. Is this true or not true? If so, how long after use can the following drugs be detected: grass, acid, DMT, hash, speed, alcohol.

Would you please answer this letter through your columns as soon as possible? Urinalysis starts next week.

Thank you,
Fearful

At the present time, there are no laboratory tests which can detect marijuana in the blood or urine. Alcohol and amphetamines (speed) can be detected by urinalysis, depending upon the amount of the drug in the body and when the urine is examined.

Nalline is the Merck Sharpe & Dohme trademark for nalorphine hydrochloride (N-allyl-normorphine hydrochloride), an antagonist to narcotics. Nalorphine is used for treatment and diagnosis.

Newborn babies of narcotic addicts are often treated with nalorphine to assist their breathing. The drug is also used to treat overdoses of narcotics in users.

When administered to a narcotic addict, nalorphine can produce severe withdrawal symptoms. This property of the drug was thought a useful way of determining narcotic use in known addicts, but reactions may be so severe (death is one) that a more humane method, urinalysis, has been found.

Directions Please

I am what you might call a semi-hip would-be pothead. Though I live in L.A. where I am probably surrounded by the stuff, I don't know where to get any. I have had one experience with pot which was very enjoyable. Could you please tell me where to get it – whom to contact or where it might grow wild? All I am interested in is pot – no LSD or bennies or anything else.

If you are interested in possessing marijuana for purposes of teaching or research, you may apply to the Internal Revenue Service, US Treasury Dept for a $1.00 marijuana tax stamp. You may be called in for an interview after which the application will be turned over to the Federal Narcotics Bureau for investigation. Your background will be thoroughly checked and very likely your home will be placed under surveillance. After many months of waiting and an exchange of letters, your application will most likely be refused whatever your qualifications or intent.

Dr Joel Fort (recently ousted from his post of Director of S.F.'s Center for Special Problems because his views of treating drug-abuse problems differed from those of the entrenched bureaucracy) possessed marijuana tax stamp M-30 in 1964, twenty-seven years after passage of the marijuana laws. Probably it was only the thirtieth such stamp issued up to that time. He believes that there are no more than ten individuals in the United States today who are permitted to do marijuana research with human subjects.

Last Chance

Dear Dr Schoenfeld:
An 80-year-old friend of ours has been hinting that he'd like to smoke some grass. We would be happy to turn him on, but only after assessing the medical advisability of doing so.

He's in perfect health mentally and physically and has no record of any outstanding problems. What do you think?
P.S. Please hurry!

In the nineteenth century, marijuana might have been touted as a 'rejuvenator' because, in common with children, its users seem to be especially sensitive to colour, sound, smell, and touch.

Tobacco and alcohol interests, who would most likely control and distribute marijuana in combustible and edible forms were it as freely available as the drugs they represent, might promote NEWPOT which 'makes you young again'. The mind boggles to think of the associated advertisements.

Certainly, there seem to be many people in their fifties and sixties who use marijuana with no apparent harmful effects. Mrs Garnet Brennan, ex-principal of the Nicasio (California) School, admitted at age 58 that she had been smoking marijuana regularly for eighteen years. But medical experience with octagenarian potheads is limited.

Your 80-year-old friend and you should also consider the legal realities as well as the medical uncertainties. I doubt that he would like to spend a large part of his remaining life in prison. If geriatric use of marijuana continues to increase we may soon see headlines like 'Senior Citizens' Center Raided' or 'Police Seize Nursing Home Inmates'.

'(AP) – A police sweep of Miami nursing homes resulted in the arrest of 458 patients, whose ages averaged 87 years. Many were apprehended as they attempted to escape in their wheelchairs. Twelve police officers were caned and several others threatened by outraged, crutch-wielding . . .'

My Son the Doctor

Dear Gene:
It has been some time since we heard from you. I hope all is well and that you are only very busy at the things you are doing.

But I do think you could spare a minute to drop us a card, that busy you're not.

The people that ask you the questions in the *Barb* must be plain nuts. It makes me sick to read the things they ask. I am surprised that something like that can go through the mail.

The man who owns the paper is just as nuts for allowing things like that to be printed in his paper.

I don't know why you waste your time on the *Barb*. You have such a gift for writing. Why don't you put it to better use?

I have been wanting to write to you for a long time how I feel about the *Barb*. I am glad I got it off my chest.

Love,
Mother

Useful References

The Art and Science of Love by Albert Ellis, PH.D. (New York: Lyle Stuart, Inc., 1965)

The Circle of Sex by Gavin Arthur (New Hyde Park: University Books, 1966)

Eros Denied: Sex in Western Society by Wayland Young (New York: Zebra Books, 1966)

Human Sexual Response by William H. Masters, MD and Virginia E. Johnson (Boston: Little, Brown and Company, 1966)

The Kama Sutra of Vatsyayana, translated by Sir Richard Burton and F. F. Arbuthnot (New York: Capricorn Books, 1963)

Sex and the Law by Morris Ploscowe (New York: Ace Books, 1962)

Sexercises – Isometric and Isotonic by Edward O'Relly (New York: Pocket Books, 1968)

Sexology, edited by Isadore Rubin, PhD (New York: Sexology Corporation, published monthly)

A Doctor Speaks on Sexual Expression in Marriage by Donald W. Hastings, MD (New York: Bantam Books, 1967)

The Drug Revolution by Joel Fort, MD (New York: The Bobbs-Merrill Co., Inc., 1969)

The Ecstatic Adventure by Ralph Metzner (New York: The Macmillan Company, 1968)

High Priest by Timothy Leary (Cleveland: World Publishing Company, 1968)

LSD: The Problem Solving Psychedelic by Peter Stafford and B. H. Golightly (New York: Award Books, 1967)

Marihuana – Myths and Realities, edited by J. L. Simmons, PhD (North Hollywood: Brandon House, 1967)

The Marihuana Papers, edited by David Solomon (New York: The Bobbs-Merrill Co., Inc., 1966)

Narcotics and the Law: A Critique of the American Experiment in Narcotic Drug Control by William B. Eldridge, Second Edition (Chicago: University of Chicago Press, 1967)

The Pharmacological Basis of Therapeutics, Goodman and Gilman, Third Edition (New York: The Macmillan Company, 1965)

Pot – A Handbook of Marijuana by John Rosevear (New Hyde Park: University Books, 1967)

The Use of LSD in Psychotherapy and Alcoholism, edited by Harold A. Abramson, MD (New York: The Bobbs-Merrill Co., Inc., 1967)

The Varieties of Psychedelic Experience by R. E. L. Masters and Jean Houston (New York: Holt, Rinehart and Winston, 1966)

Index